The Grapes of Wrath

JOHN STEINBECK

Level 5

Retold by Paola Trimarco
Series Editors: Andy Hopkins and Jocelyn Potter

Pearson Education Limited
Edinburgh Gate, Harlow,
Essex CM20 2JE, England
and Associated Companies throughout the world.

ISBN: 978-1-4058-6251-6

First published in the UK in 1939 by William Heinemann Ltd
First Penguin Books edition published 2001
This edition published 2008

16

Typeset by Graphicraft Ltd, Hong Kong
Set in 11/14pt Bembo
Printed in China
SWTC/16

Published by Pearson Education Ltd

For a complete list of the titles available in the Pearson English Readers series, please visit www.pearsonenglishreaders.com. Alternatively, write to your local Pearson Education office or to Pearson English Readers Marketing Department, Pearson Education, Edinburgh Gate, Harlow, Essex CM20 2JE, England.

Contents

Introduction

Uncle John said, "We've never been paupers before."

"Maybe we have to learn," Tom said. "We never were forced off our land before."

In the 1920s, Americans experienced a period of economic growth and life was full of promise. But on October 24, 1929, the center of finance in the United States, Wall Street, crashed. The economy failed and money lost value rapidly. No one was prepared. Shockwaves affected the banking system all over the country.

This was the start of the Great Depression, which lasted through the 1930s. During those years, there was less business activity and there was high unemployment. By 1933, sixteen million Americans—twenty-five percent of the working population—were unemployed. Across the country, banks closed down and people lost their savings.

In many towns and cities around the country, people soon had no money and became homeless. People who had been rich were suddenly desperate. Some people killed themselves. Farmers, factory workers, and others traveled west looking for work in California. They filled their cars and trucks with things they needed for the long trip. They had to leave their homes and many of their possessions, which was often heartbreaking. At night the travelers stopped to rest and strangers found themselves living together in camps. These camps were called Hoovervilles because a lot of people blamed President Hoover for the Depression. They were often dirty and dangerous places, where some people lived in boxes and others in cars or tents.

At the same time, the southwestern states (including Oklahoma,

Kansas, and Arkansas) were suffering from a lack of rain. In these states, the land dried and turned to dust. It was impossible to grow fruit or vegetables. Cattle dropped dead. People did, too. These states became known as the Dust Bowl.

Feeling the economic pressure, the banks in the Dust Bowl states were unable to save the land. They forced the tenant farmers off their farms. Hundreds of thousands of people left the Dust Bowl and headed west to California. These people heard that California was the golden state—the land of jobs, green hills, and valleys of fruit trees. They drove thousands of miles in search of work and a better life for their families. They did not know that these promises of jobs were lies.

Along the way, whole families became migrant workers, working hard for very little money. They picked fruit, vegetables, and cotton. The children couldn't go to school and there wasn't much food, so their education and health suffered. As they lived among strangers in these difficult circumstances, their young eyes were opened to a world of troubles and pain. But these children also learned about sharing with others and helping their neighbors. Many of the poor people were very generous to others who had even less than they did.

The government money that was supposed to help the migrant families often went into the pockets of local officials. There were plenty of greedy policemen and sheriffs who made life very difficult for the poor. They wanted to take everything from them that they could. After they got what they wanted, they drove the families out of their state. Nobody wanted paupers.

When these people arrived in California, they did not find good, well paid jobs. Californians did not want them in their state. They called these people from Oklahoma and the other Dust Bowl states "Oakies"—people who were poor, uneducated, and unwanted. Californians attacked their southwestern speech, their strange food, their poor clothes, and their country music.

Steinbeck's story of the Joad family's struggle during the Depression shines a light on this dark period in America's history. Putting everything they own into their old truck, the Joad family leaves Oklahoma for California. They have been tenant farmers for many years. Before the Depression started and the lack of rain dried up the land, they had worked hard and had earned enough money to live simple lives. Although they were never rich, they were never paupers—until now. The Joads are forced to learn a new way of life on the road with little money.

Ma and Pa are the heads of the Joad family. One of their sons, Tom, has just been freed from prison and is on parole. Their eldest son, Noah, a strange boy, has always been slow and quiet. Their teenage son, Al, is more interested in girls than anything else. But he has learned about cars and this is useful for the family. Their daughter, Rosasharn, has recently married Connie Rivers and is now expecting their first child. The youngest Joad children, Ruthie and Winfield, are too young to understand everything that is happening. To them, this new life is a big adventure.

Other members of the Joad family on this journey to California include Grandma, Grandpa, and Uncle John. The grandparents are old and it breaks their hearts to leave their home. The family is joined by Casy, who has been a preacher until the Depression makes him question his religion.

On the road to California, the family struggles with illness and death. They meet people who say that life in California is hard and that people are dying of hunger there. But the Joads' hopes for jobs and a better future keep them going. There is nothing to go back to.

Ma's love for her husband and children helps them through many difficult times. Often unable to give them the food they need, she feeds them her strength and constant hope for a brighter future. Hope will see them through to their final destination, she thinks. Although they are often discouraged and hungry, Ma never gives up. At the end of the story, she is proud of her daughter, Rosasharn, when she performs an unselfish act of kindness toward a complete stranger.

Steinbeck wrote the novel in the language of the migrant workers, using words like "ain't," which are avoided by educated Americans. Other words like "Ma" for mother and "Pa" for father are common in the southwest but are often laughed at by Americans from other states. The words "folks" and "fellow" are less formal words for people and man and suggest friends rather than strangers.

John Steinbeck was born in Salinas, California, on February 27, 1902. His family was middle-class and he went to Stanford University, with breaks, from 1919 to 1925. Although he hoped to become a journalist, he never finished his degree in English. Before he became a successful writer, he had many different jobs. He was a ranch worker, a fruit picker, and a builder. His realistic descriptions of the lives of workers in his novels grew out of the people he met in these jobs.

Later, he worked for the *San Francisco News*, reporting on the lives of farm workers. Their stories gave Steinbeck ideas for *The Grapes of Wrath*, which was published in 1939. The book won the 1940 Pulitzer Prize and made many people realize how hard the lives of poor farm workers really were.

Although today it is considered a great America novel, not everybody liked *The Grapes of Wrath* in 1939. It told some ugly truths that a lot of people wanted to keep secret. Some government officials said it was full of lies. Some school officials refused to allow students to read it in schools. Steinbeck grew very worried about the negative attention his book received. When he moved to Monterey, California people didn't want to rent him office space where he could write more novels. In 1944, it is reported that he said, "This isn't my country any more. It makes me very sad."

But in 1940, *The Grapes of Wrath* was made into a movie, directed by John Ford and starring Henry Fonda as Tom Joad. Steinbeck's other famous works include *Tortilla Flat* (1935), *Of Mice and Men* (1937), *The Pearl* (1949), *The Red Pony* (1948), and *East of Eden* (1952). All of these books were also made into movies.

Steinbeck won many prizes for his novels and was given the Nobel Prize for Literature in 1962. Today he is remembered because he told real stories about real people. He understood the idea of "the American dream," but he knew that it was not possible for everyone. He wrote in a clear and simple style. And he wrote about the poor and homeless people who many people wished to forget.

Steinbeck had three wives and he had two sons with his second wife. He died in New York on December 20, 1968. The National Steinbeck Center in Salinas, California celebrates his life and work. You can also find a lot of information about Steinbeck and his novels on the Internet.

Chapter 1 Tom Comes Home

The clouds appeared, but went away again. It seemed they did not even try to make rain. The surface of the earth had formed a dry hard layer. The dirt layer broke and the dust formed. Every moving thing—a walking man, a wagon, a car—lifted the dust into the air. People stayed in their houses, and they tied cloth over their noses and wore glasses to protect their eyes when they went out.

A great red truck stood in front of a little roadside diner. Inside, the truck driver sat on a chair and rested his elbows on the counter and looked over his coffee at the lean and lonely waitress. Outside, a man who was walking along the highway crossed over and approached the truck. He stopped in front of it and read the *No Riders* sign on the windshield.

The man outside was close to thirty. His eyes were dark brown and his cheeks were high and wide. He wore a new gray suit but it was cheap. His gray cap was so new that it was still stiff.

In the diner, the truck driver paid his bill. He was a heavy red-faced man with broad shoulders and a thick stomach. He stepped outside and walked to the big red truck.

The man in the cheap gray suit asked, "Could you give me a lift, sir?"

"Didn't you see the *No Riders* sign on the windshield?"

"I sure did, but my feet are really tired."

"New shoes," the truck driver said, looking down at them. "You shouldn't walk in new shoes in hot weather."

"I don't have any other shoes," the hitchhiker said.

"Well, OK then."

"Thanks."

The hitchhiker opened the door and slid into the seat. The driver looked at him carefully, then started the engine.

"Are you going far?" the driver asked.

"No."

"Looking for a job?"

"No, my pa's got a place. He's a tenant farmer and we've been there a long time."

"A tenant farmer and he's still here?"

"Of course, I ain't heard lately."

The driver then asked, "Have you been at a job?"

"I sure have," the hitchhiker said.

"I thought so. I see your hands. They look like they've been swinging a hammer."

"Would you like to know anything else? I'll tell you. My name's Tom Joad. My pa is old Tom Joad. And you know where I just came from, don't you!"

"Now, don't get angry. That ain't my business," the driver said nervously.

"Well, I'll tell you. Yeah, I was in prison."

"It ain't my business," the driver said weakly.

"See that road up ahead?" Tom asked.

"Yeah."

"Well, I get off there."

Soon the truck stopped. Tom thanked the driver and the truck went off.

Tom took off his coat and then his shoes. He wrapped the shoes in the coat and placed them under his arm. At last, he walked up the side road through the fields with a cloud of dust following behind him.

Then he saw a man sitting under a tree. The man wore old jeans and a blue shirt. His shoes, gray with dust, lay on the ground in front of him.

Tom stopped in the shade and wiped his face with his cap. "Hi, it's hotter than hell out here."

The seated man stared at Tom. "Now, ain't you young Tom Joad?"

"Yeah. Going home now."

"You probably don't remember me," the man said. "I was the preacher, Reverend Jim Casy. Just Jim Casy now."

"Sure, I remember you," Tom said. "You used to give a good service."

"Well, I ain't preaching now. The spirit ain't in people. Worse than that, the spirit ain't in me," he said sadly. "It's a funny thing, but I was just thinking about old Tom Joad when you came along. I was thinking I should visit him. How is your old pa?"

"I don't know how he is. I ain't been home in four years."

"Didn't he write to you?"

Tom was embarrassed. "Well, Pa never did write letters. He could write his name all right, but he never wrote letters to people."

"So, have you been traveling around?" Casy asked.

Tom looked strangely at Casy. "Didn't you hear about me? It was in all the papers."

"No. What happened?"

Tom said pleasantly, "Well . . ." He paused for a moment and then said, "I've been in McAlester for four years."

"I won't ask you any questions if you've done something bad."

"I'd do it again," Tom said. "I killed a guy in a fight. We were drunk at a dance. He put a knife in me, so I killed him with a shovel. I got seven years for that. I got out in four. I'm out on parole."

"So, you ain't heard anything about your family in four years."

"Just a couple of Christmas cards from Ma and Grandma."

"Your pa's house is about a mile from here. Let's go," Casy said as he got up from under the tree.

The two men hesitated on the edge of the shade, then walked out into the yellow sunlight. The path led them through fields of dusty green cotton.

The sun was lower in the sky when Tom pointed to a fence and said, "There's our line."

They moved over the top of a hill and saw the Joad place below them. Tom stopped. "It ain't the same," he said. "Look at that house. Something happened. There ain't anyone there."

The Reverend Casy and young Tom stood on the hill and stared down at the small unpainted house.

Casy said, "Let's look in the house. It's all pushed out of shape. If I was still a preacher, I'd say the arm of God had struck. But now I don't know what happened."

They walked down to the front of the house and Tom said, "They're gone, or Ma's dead." He pointed to the low gate across the front door. "If Ma was anywhere near, the gate would be shut and hooked."

The sun had lowered until it shone through the windows, and it flashed on the edges of the broken glass. Tom Joad turned at last and crossed the porch. He rolled a cigarette, smoothed it, and lighted it. He breathed in deeply and blew the smoke out through his nose. "Something's wrong," he said.

The preacher stared across the fields. "Somebody's coming. Look!"

"I can't see him because of the dust he's raising. Who is that?" The man came closer and, as he walked past the barn, Tom said, "Oh, I know him. You know him, Casy—that's Muley Graves." Then he called out, "Hey, Muley! How are you?"

The man stopped, and then he walked quickly. He was a lean man, fairly short. His movements were nervous and quick. He wore blue jeans that were thin at the knee and seat and an old black suit coat that was spotted with dirt.

"Who's that?" the man called. Muley came very close before he recognized the faces. "Well . . ." he said. "It's Tommy Joad. When did you get out, Tommy?"

"Two days ago," said Tom. "It took a little time to hitchhike home. And look what I find. Where are my folks, Muley? And why is the house destroyed?"

"By God, it's lucky that I came by!" said Muley. "Yeah, old Tom was worried about you coming home and finding nobody."

"But where are my folks?" Tom asked nervously.

"Well, it took three trips with your Uncle John's wagon. They're all at your Uncle John's," Muley said.

"Oh! All at John's. Well, what are they doing there?"

"They've been picking cotton, all of them, even the kids and your grandpa. They're getting money together so they can go out west. They're going to buy a car and go out west where it's easy living. There's nothing here."

Tom asked, "They ain't gone yet?"

"No," Muley said. "But the last I heard was four days ago."

"OK," said Tom. "You know the preacher here, Reverend Casy."

"Sure, sure," Muley said. "Glad to see you again," he said to Casy. The two men shook hands. "Where have you been these days?" he asked.

"I've been away asking questions," said Casy. "But, what happened here? Why did they force folks off the land?"

"The dust came up and spoiled everything, and the folks who owned the land said, 'We can't afford to keep tenants.' So they came with tractors and pushed all the tenants off the land. All except me."

A large red drop of sun fell over the horizon and was gone.

Tom said, "Well, we ain't going to walk eight miles to Uncle John's place tonight. My feet are sore. Can we go to your place, Muley? It's only about a half mile away."

Muley seemed embarrassed. "My wife and kids and her brother all left and went to California. There wasn't anything to eat here."

"And you didn't go?" Casy asked. "Why didn't you stay with your family?"

Muley said, "I couldn't go. Something wouldn't let me."

"Well, I'm hungry," said Tom. "Do you have anything to eat, Muley? How have you been getting your dinner?"

Muley said, looking ashamed, "At first I ate mice. I had to. But now I've made traps and I catch rabbits and wild chickens." He reached into his sack and three dead rabbits came falling out.

"Well, it's more than four years since I ate fresh-killed meat," said Tom. He rubbed his hands together. "Who's got a knife?"

Muley gave Tom his pocket knife and Tom prepared the rabbits. They made a fire from some broken wood from the house. Then Tom put the pieces of meat on a wire that they found in the barn and turned them over the fire.

After the three men finished eating, the preacher stood up and said slowly, "Yeah, I'm going with you, Tom. And when your folks are out on the road, I'll go with them."

"You're welcome," said Tom. "Do you think you'll come along, Muley?"

"What? No, I'm not going anywhere," Muley said. He was staring out ahead. "Do you see that beam of light moving over there? That's probably the man in charge of this piece of land. Somebody saw our fire."

Tom looked. A beam of light was coming from over the hill. "But we ain't doing anything. We're just sitting here."

Muley laughed. "Yeah, we're doing something just being here. We're trespassing. We can't stay. They've been trying to catch me for two months."

"What's wrong with you, Muley?" Tom asked. "You never were the type of person to run and hide."

stood in the yard, a strange truck. The front was a car, but the top had been cut off in the middle and a bed fitted on.

Tom moved forward and leaned against the truck. His father looked at him, but did not see him. He was busy nailing some wood together to make the truck sides. Tom noticed that he had become older and grayer. He said softly, "Pa."

"What do you want?" his father spoke around the nails he had pressed between his lips. He was a short lean man and wore a dirty black hat and a blue work shirt. His jeans were held up by an old leather belt that was ragged from years of wear. He held his hammer in the air and was ready to hit a nail into the wood when he realized who it was. His mouth opened, and the nails fell from his mouth. A look of fear came into his eyes. "Tommy," he said softly. "Did you escape? Do you have to hide?" He listened closely.

"No," said Tom. "I'm paroled. I'm free. I have my papers."

Pa dropped the hammer. He felt embarrassed and strange. "Tommy," he said, "we're going to California, and we were going to write and tell you. But now you're back and you can go with us!" His eyes were bright with excitement. But then they grew sad. "Can you go with us, Tom? Will you break your parole if you leave the state?"

"Only if they know I left," Tom said. "Then I'd get sent back to McAlester. But if they don't know, there's no problem. We can't stay here."

"Ma will be so happy. She was worried that she'd never see you again." He then smiled at his son. "Let's surprise her." At last, he touched Tom, but only on the shoulder. He looked at Jim Casy.

Tom said, "You remember the preacher, Pa. He came along with me."

"Has he been in prison, too?"

"No, I met him on the road. He's been away."

Pa shook Casy's hand. "You're welcome here, sir."

Casy said, "I'm glad to be here. It's a thing to see when a boy comes home."

"Come on," Pa said, walking quickly to the house. "I can't wait to see the look on her face when she sees you."

Pa stepped into the doorway and stood there to block it with his body. He said, "Ma, there are a couple of fellows here and they need some food."

"Let them in. We have plenty. But tell them they have to wash their hands."

Pa walked away from the doorway, and Tom looked in at his mother. She turned toward the door, but the sun was behind Tom and she only saw a dark figure with sunlight around it. "Come in," she said warmly.

Tom continued to look. Ma was heavy but not fat. She was thick from having children and work. Her old dress, with colors that had been washed out, came down to her ankles. Pa stood near Tom and shook with excitement. "Come right in, sir," he said with a broad smile.

Ma looked up again pleasantly from the frying pan. Then her hand dropped slowly to her side and the fork fell to the wooden floor. Her eyes opened wide. She breathed heavily through her opened mouth. Then she closed her eyes. "Thank God," she said. "Oh, thank God!" But then, suddenly, her face looked worried. "Tommy, you ain't wanted by the police? You didn't escape?"

"No, Ma. Parole. I have the papers right here," he said, touching his pocket.

Ma moved toward him soundlessly. Her small hand felt his arm and then her fingers went up to his cheek as a blind person's fingers might. "Well," she cried. "We almost left without you. We were wondering how in the world you were going to find us."

"Well, I'm back now, Ma."

She smiled gently and returned to preparing the meal.

Tom asked, "Where's Grandpa? I ain't seen the old devil."

Ma placed the plates on the table. "Oh, he and Grandma sleep in the barn because they get up so much during the night." Then she looked at Pa. "Pa, run outside and tell Grandma and Grandpa that Tommy's home."

"Of course," said Pa as he went out the door.

"Ma, when I saw what they did to our house . . ."

She moved up closely to Tom and said, "Now, don't you go fighting them alone. They'll hunt you down like a wild animal."

Across the yard came four people. Grandpa was ahead. He was a lean, ragged, quick old man. Behind him was Grandma, who wore an old housedress that she pulled above her knees as she walked. The two old people raced each other to get across the yard. They fought over everything and loved and needed the fighting. Behind them were Pa and Noah—Noah, the firstborn child, tall and strange, always with a puzzled look on his face. He moved slowly and rarely spoke.

Grandpa demanded, "Where is he?" Then he saw Tom standing in the door.

Grandma suddenly cried, "Praise God!"

Grandpa walked up and hit Tom on the chest, and his eyes smiled with love and pride. "How are you, Tommy?"

"OK," said Tom.

Noah stood on the step and looked at Tom. His face had little expression. Tom said, "How are you, Noah?"

"Fine," said Noah. "How are you?" That was all, but it was a comfortable thing.

Suddenly Tom said, "Hey! Where's the preacher? He was right here. Where did he go?"

Pa said, "I saw him, but he's gone."

Tom stepped out onto the porch and called out, "Jim, Jim Casy!" The preacher appeared from behind the barn and walked over to the house. "Come on in and eat," said Tom.

They all ate quickly, and there was no talk until the food was gone and the coffee drunk. Then Tom and Pa stepped outside and looked at the truck.

Pa said, "Your brother, Al, looked it over before we bought it. He says it's all right."

"What does that little kid know?"

"He worked for a company and drove a truck last year. He knows a little. And he's sixteen now," Pa explained.

Tom asked, "Where is he?"

"Well," said Pa, "he's out chasing girls again. That's all he thinks about, girls and engines."

"Where's Uncle John? And where's Rosasharn and Ruthie and Winfield?" Tom asked. "Nobody said anything about them yet."

"Nobody asked," said Pa. "Ruthie and Winfield went into town with John early this morning to sell a load of stuff. Rosasharn is staying with Connie and his folks. Oh, you don't even know. Rosasharn's married to Connie Rivers, and she's going to have a baby in four or five months."

"Jesus!" said Tom. "Rosasharn was just a little kid when I last saw her and now she's going to have a baby!" He smiled at the thought. "And when are we going to start out west, Pa?"

"Well, we need to sell some more stuff first. We ain't got a lot of money. This man I know said that it's two thousand miles to California. Do you have any money?"

"Just a couple of dollars. How did you get money?"

"Well," said Pa, "we sold stuff and then we picked cotton, even Grandpa." He looked at his son. "Did you spend your money on those new clothes?"

"No, Pa. They gave them to me. I drove a truck at McAlester. I could drive if you need me to."

"Good," said Pa. "Hey, there's that little brother of yours coming up the road."

Tom looked up the road. He saw Al in stiff jeans and high boots walking proudly toward them. When Al got near, he recognized Tom's face and his face lit up. Tom said, "Wow, Al! You've grown like a bean!" Tom put out his hand and Al shook it hard and fast.

Tom stayed in the house that morning and talked to Ma, while Pa and Al drove into town to sell more tools and furniture and to pick up the others. Casy went out for one last walk in the fields.

Ma said, "Tom, I hope things are good in California."

Tom turned to her. "What makes you think they ain't?" he asked.

"Well, nothing. I guess it seems too nice. I've seen handbills being passed out, saying that there are jobs and high wages. And I've seen in the newspaper that they want people to pick grapes, oranges, and peaches. Won't that be great, Tom—picking peaches?"

Tom watched her working in the kitchen, and his eyes smiled at her. "That does sound good, Ma. But I met a fellow who said that too many folks are looking for work right now. And he says the folks that pick the fruit live in dirty camps and hardly get enough to eat."

"Oh, no. That ain't so," Ma said. "Your father got a handbill saying that they need folks to work. They wouldn't bother making all those handbills if it weren't true."

"I sure hope you're right, Ma."

In the late afternoon, the truck came back in a cloud of dust. The children—Ruthie, the twelve-year-old, and Winfield, the ten-year-old—stood in the back. Beside them, holding onto the bars of the truck was blond-haired Rosasharn, who was thinking about the baby and being careful. In recent weeks, she had become shy and thoughtful as she worried about becoming a mother. Her nineteen-year-old husband, Connie, a sharp-faced and lean young man, was proud and afraid of the change in her.

When the truck stopped, Ruthie and Winfield climbed over the bar screaming, "Where is he? Where's Tom?" Then they saw him standing beside the door and stopped suddenly and walked slowly and shyly toward him.

"Hello. How are you kids doing?" he asked.

"Hello! All right," they replied softly.

Then Tom said, "Hey, it's Rosasharn."

She smiled sweetly at her brother and said proudly, "This is Connie Rivers, my husband."

The two young men shook hands.

The rest of the day was spent loading the truck. In the evening they killed and cooked the last pig. Then they salted the pieces of meat for the journey. With the children in bed, the adults gathered together on the porch to make their plans.

Pa drew numbers in the dust and whispered to himself. He finally looked up and said, "One hundred and fifty-four dollars. That's what we have." Pa shook his head. "They say it's two thousand miles to California. We should go soon."

Tom said, "Well, if we work all night, we could be ready to leave in the morning."

Tom helped Ma pack the kitchen and the meat, while Pa and Noah put clothes and tools into boxes and Casy helped Al prepare the truck.

The early morning sunlight was suddenly in the sky. Rosasharn and the children were woken first. With tired faces, they climbed into the truck. Then, when everything was ready, they woke up Grandma and Grandpa.

Grandpa's eyes were dull. He said in a loud voice, "Well, I ain't going!"

"Not going?" said Pa. "What do you mean? There's no place to stay."

"I'm staying," the old man said. "This is my country. I belong here. I don't want any stupid oranges or grapes. This is where I've always lived and this is where I'm going to stay!"

"Oh, Grandpa," Ma said. "We have to go. Sit down and have coffee with us."

Pa and Tom gave Ma a strange look.

Grandpa sat down, still protesting, and Ma prepared the coffee. To Grandpa's cup she added some strong cough medicine. The family watched as he drank his coffee and ate his pork. They saw him yawn and then rest his head on his arms and go to sleep. Then Tom and Al lifted him up onto the truck and laid him on top of the load.

The rest of the family and Casy got into the truck or on the back. Al started the engine, and as the truck slowly went up the little hill, he said, "What a load! We won't be able to go very fast."

The people on top of the load looked back and saw the house and the barn and a little smoke still rising from the chimney. The truck moved slowly through the dust toward the highway and the west.

Chapter 3 Highway 66

Highway 66 was the main route for a people in flight from dust and empty land. All day the cars and trucks filled with families and everything they owned streamed along the road.

Al was at the wheel, a serious look on his face, his whole body listening to the truck for weaknesses. Grandma sat next to him half asleep. Ma sat next to Grandma with one elbow out the window. Suddenly Grandma said, "I have to get out."

"OK," Al said. The truck came to a stop at the side of the road. Ma and Grandma got out first. Then the others in the back came to life and jumped out. Grandpa stayed in the truck.

"Ain't you going to come out, Grandpa?" Tom asked.

"No, I ain't going, I'm telling you," Grandpa said angrily. "I'm going to stay here like old Muley Graves." The old man then folded his arms.

"Tom," Ma called out. "Get that food out. We need to eat something." Tom found a pan of pork bones and passed them around.

Then Winfield said, "I want a drink."

Then Ruthie said, "Yeah, me too."

Al felt his fear growing. "We'll get water at the first gas station we come to. We need gas as well." The family agreed and quickly got back in. Al started the motor and they moved on.

It was another twenty miles before they saw a gas station. Everyone was thirsty and tired. Al pulled the truck into the station and a heavy man got up from a chair behind the gas pumps. "Are you folks going to buy anything? Gas or stuff?" he asked.

"We need some gas, sir," Al said.

"Do you have any money?"

"Of course we do. We're not begging."

"Well, that's all right then. Help yourself to water." Then he explained, "This road is full of people. They come in, use water, dirty the restrooms, and then they steal stuff. They don't have any money to buy anything. Some come here begging for a gallon of gas."

Tom moved angrily toward the man. "We're paying our own way," he said in an angry voice. "We ain't asking for anything."

The man stepped back. "Just help yourself to water, and the restrooms are out back."

Winfield ran to the water and drank hurriedly and then poured some over his head and face. The man watched him with a smile. He then looked at Tom and Al. "Over fifty cars a day have been stopping here. All these folks are moving west. Where are they going? What are they going to do?"

"They're doing the same thing as we are. Looking for work. Trying to feed our families. That's all," Tom said.

"Well, I'm just trying to run a business here. These folks come by and beg for gas, and then they give me stuff for the gas. I can show you beds and baby toys and pots and pans." He picked up the gas line and brought it to the truck. "I just don't know what this country is coming to. What's happening to people?"

Casy had been listening to the man. "I've been walking around this country," Casy said. "And I've heard a lot of folks asking the same questions. Well, people are moving. They're moving because they have to."

Over by the water, Connie and Rosasharn stood together, talking secretly. Connie washed a tin cup and filled it with water. He said, "If there's a lot of work in California, we can get our own car. Maybe we can get a house."

"I'd like to have a car," Rosasharn said. "But the house would come first."

"Of course, a house would come first," he said, looking at his new wife. "Are you all right?"

"Tired. I'm just tired from riding in the sun."

"We have to do that or we won't get to California."

"I know," she said.

Then Tom called out, "Come on, everyone. We have to go. We have lots of driving to do."

"Now, where are those kids?" Pa asked. "Winfield! Ruthie!" he called out. Then he whistled.

Tom asked Al, "Do you want me to drive?"

Al said, "OK. But watch the oil and drive it slowly. This truck is overloaded."

The truck drove along slowly and the sun lowered in the sky in front of them. The sign said Oklahoma City. Tom drove straight on. The outskirts were wide spread. Tom drove carefully in the traffic, and then they were on 66—the great western road—again and the sun was sinking on the line of the road.

Tom said, "We stay on this road all the way."

Ma had been silent for a long time. "Maybe we'd better find a place to stop before sunset," she said. "I have to get some pork boiling and some bread made."

"Sure," Tom agreed. "We ain't going to make this trip in one jump."

"Yeah, got to get some supper cooking." And then she said, "Tom, I'm scared about you crossing the state line. Maybe they'll catch you."

Tom held his hand over his eyes to protect himself from the brightness of the sun. "Don't you worry," he said. "There're lots of fellows out on parole and there are more going into jail all the time. If I get caught for anything else out west, well, then they have my picture and my fingerprints in Washington. They'll send me back. But if I don't do any crimes, they won't notice me."

"I'm still scared about it. Sometimes you do a crime and you don't even know it. Maybe they have crimes in California we don't even know about."

"Stop worrying, Ma."

"I can't help it," she said. "The minute you cross the line you've done a crime."

"Well, it's better than staying in Oklahoma and dying of

hunger," he said. "We need to look for a place to stop." Then he pointed ahead. "There're some folks camping. It looks like a good place to me."

He slowed the truck and stopped beside the road. A middle-aged man stood looking down at the motor of his old car. His face was thin and his chin stood out sharply. Tom leaned out of the window. "Any law against folks stopping here for the night?"

The man looked at Tom. "I don't know," he said. "We only stopped here because of this old car."

"Any water here?"

The man pointed to a little house in the distance. "There's water there."

Tom said, "Well, can we camp here with you? You have a right to say if you want neighbors or not."

The thin man's face smiled. "Sure, come on off the road. We're happy to have you." Then he called, "Sairy, there are some folks here that are going to stay with us." He looked at Tom and added, "Sairy ain't well."

The tent opened and a small woman came out. Her face was tired and dry. When she spoke, her voice was beautiful and soft. "Tell them welcome," she said.

Tom drove off the road and brought the truck into the field beside the car. The family quickly jumped out of the truck. Ma went speedily to work.

The man said, "I'm Wilson, Ivy Wilson."

"We're Joads," said Pa.

"Glad to meet you," Mr. Wilson said.

Noah and Uncle John and the preacher began to unload the truck. They helped Grandpa down and sat him on the ground. The old man sat, staring ahead. "Are you sick, Grandpa?" Noah asked.

"Yeah, I'm sick," Grandpa said weakly.

Sairy Wilson walked slowly and carefully toward him. "How would you like to come into our tent? You could lie down and rest."

Without warning, Grandpa began to cry. Ma lifted him to his feet and then helped him into the tent.

Uncle John said, "He must be real sick. He's never done that before. I've never seen him cry in his life."

Ma came out of the tent and went to Casy. "You've been around sick people," she said. "Please go take a look at Grandpa."

Casy walked quickly to the tent and went inside. He took the bony old wrist into his fingers. "Feeling tired, Grandpa?"

The old man made sounds that were not words.

Ma looked into the tent. "Grandma wants to come in. Do you think he's all right?"

Casy shook his head slowly.

Ma said, "He's all right, Grandma. He's just taking a rest."

Grandma answered, "Well, I want to see him." She came running into the tent and looked down at her old husband. "What's the matter with you?" she asked Grandpa.

Casy said gently, "He's sick, Grandma."

"Oh." She looked down at the old man again. "Sick bad, do you think?"

"Pretty sick, Grandma."

The people outside the tent were standing quietly, listening to the sounds of dying.

Casy looked into Grandpa's eyes. They were clear and deep and there was a knowing peaceful look about them. Then, Grandpa's breathing stopped.

Sairy took Grandma by the arm and led her outside and Grandma moved with pride and held her head high.

Casy stepped out of the tent. The family sat together on the ground. Pa was the head of the family now. He looked at Casy and said, "What are we going to do? There are laws. You have to report a death, and when you do that, they either take forty dollars or they think he's a pauper."

Uncle John said, "We've never been paupers before."

"Maybe we have to learn," Tom said. "We never were forced off our land before."

"No. We'll wait for it to get darker, and we'll bury Grandpa ourselves," Pa said.

On the edge of the ring of firelight the men gathered. Pa marked out a place on the ground eight feet long and three feet wide. When they finished digging the large hole, Ma pulled a clear page out of the front of the Bible and handed it to Tom. He took a pencil out of his pocket and wrote, "This is William James Joad, died an old, old man. His folks buried him because they didn't have enough money for a funeral. Nobody killed him."

After the men buried Grandpa and covered the hole with dirt, the two families sat around the fire eating the pork and potatoes. They were all quiet, staring into the fire.

Then Pa said to Mr. Wilson, "How long have you folks been on the road?"

Wilson cleared his teeth with his tongue and swallowed. "We ain't been lucky. We've been away from home three weeks."

"Well, we plan to be in California in ten days or less."

Al said, "I don't know, Pa. With the load we're carrying, we'll be lucky to get there at all. Not if there are mountains to go over."

Ma said, "Rosasharn, go lie down with Grandma. She needs somebody now."

Rosasharn got to her feet and walked to the old bed and lay beside Grandma. The two whispered together.

Al said, "It's a shame about Grandpa. Before we left, he was talking about what he was going to do in California."

"He was pretending all the time," Casy said. "I think he knew. He didn't die tonight. He died the minute you took him off the place."

"Are you sure of that?" Pa cried.

"Oh, he was breathing, but he was dead. He was that place, and he knew it."

Uncle John asked, "You knew he was dying?"

Casy said, "Yeah, but we couldn't do anything. We had to go and he knew it. And he didn't suffer. He's just staying with the land. He couldn't leave it."

Wilson said, "Yeah, we had to leave my brother Will. He couldn't leave the land, and we couldn't wait. So, we went one hundred miles when the car broke down. It cost thirty dollars to get it fixed. And then we had to get a tire, and then Sairy got sick. Had to stop for ten days. And now the car's broken again and money's getting low. I don't know when we'll ever get to California. If I could only fix a car, but I don't know anything about cars."

"What's the matter with it?" Al asked.

"Runs a minute, and then stops."

Al spoke proudly. "I think you have a blocked gas line. I'll blow it out for you."

And Pa was proud, too. "He's good with a car."

"Well, thank you for your help," Wilson said to Al. "Yeah, when we get to California we'll buy a new car that doesn't break down."

"When we get there," Pa said. "The problem is getting there."

"Oh, but it'll be worth it," said Wilson. "I've seen handbills that say they need folks for picking and for good wages. They don't care how much you eat because they have plenty. And I bet in a couple of years a fellow could have a place of his own."

Pa said, "We've seen those handbills. I have one right here." He took out his wallet and unfolded an orange handbill. In black type it said: "Pea Pickers Wanted in California. Good Wages All Season. 800 Pickers Wanted."

Wilson looked at it curiously. "That's the one I've seen. The exact same one. Do you suppose they have all eight hundred already?"

Pa said, "This is just one little part of California. There are plenty of other places."

Then Tom said, "I've been thinking. We have an overloaded truck, but Mr. and Mrs. Wilson don't. If some of us could ride with them and take some of their light stuff in the truck, we could get up hills. We'd keep together on the road and it would be good for everybody."

Wilson jumped up. "Sure. That would be great. Did you hear that, Sairy?"

"It's a nice thing," Sairy said. "I hope we aren't troubling you folks."

"You'd be helping us," Pa said.

Ma said, "You helped us with Grandpa. Now we'll help you." The relationship was plain.

Al cried, "That car will easily take six."

Sairy said, "If I get sick again, you have to go on and get there."

Ma looked carefully at Sairy and said, "We're going to see that you get through."

Sairy stared into the firelight. "We have to get some sleep tonight." She stood up.

"Grandpa—it's like he's been dead a year," Ma said sadly.

The families moved lazily to their sleep. Only Sairy Wilson lay awake. She stared into the sky and held her body firmly against the pain.

Chapter 4 Mechanical Problems

Joads and Wilsons slowly moved west along 66 as a team. That night they ate only pieces of bread, cold and hard, left from breakfast. For two days, the families were in flight, out of Oklahoma and across Texas. Al drove the car, and his mother sat beside him and Rosasharn beside her. The Wilsons sat quietly in the back. "Ma," the girl said, "when we get there, all of you are going to pick fruit and live in the country, ain't you?"

Ma smiled. "We ain't there yet. We don't know what it's like."

"Me and Connie don't want to live in the country," the girl said. "We have it all planned."

For a moment a little worry came on Ma's face. "Ain't you going to stay with us—with the family?"

"Well, Connie and me talked about it. Ma, we want to live in a town." She went on excitedly. "Connie's going to get a job in a store or maybe a factory. And he's going to study at home. And maybe later he'll have his own store. And we'll go to the movies whenever we want." Her face shone with excitement. "And when Connie gets his store, Al could work for him."

Ma said, "We don't want you to go away from us. It ain't good for folks to break up."

Al said, "Me work for Connie? How about Connie working for me?"

A noise could be heard in the engine. Al speeded up and the banging noise grew louder. He drove the car to the side of the road. Tom stopped the truck close to the car and jumped out. "What's the matter, Al?"

"Listen to this," Al said. He turned on the engine and a loud banging sound filled the air.

Tom listened. "That doesn't sound good."

"I kept plenty of oil in there."

"Well, it's all dry now," Tom said. "And we'll have to change that part." He pointed with his finger.

Al whispered angrily to himself. He drove the car into the shade and shut down the engine.

The Wilsons and the Joads slowly got out of the truck and the car. Wilson said, "It's all my fault. This stupid car has been trouble from the start. You folks have been nice to us. You just pack up and get along. Sairy and I will stay here."

Pa said slowly, "We ain't going to do that. We're almost family. Grandpa died in your tent."

Sairy said tiredly, "We've only been trouble."

Tom slowly made a cigarette and lighted it. He took off his ruined cap and wiped his forehead. "I have an idea," he said. "The nearer we get to California, the quicker we can be earning money. Now this car will go twice as fast as that truck. You take some of the stuff out of the truck, and then all of you folks can move on and Casy and I will stay and fix this car. And then we'll drive on, day and night, and we'll catch up with you. If you get through first, you'll be working and things will be easy."

The family considered it. Pa scratched the earth with his finger. "I think Tom's right," he said. "It's no good for all of us to stay here. We can get fifty, a hundred miles before dark."

Ma said worriedly, "How are you going to find us?"

"We'll be on the same road," said Tom. "Sixty-six all the way. Go to a place called Bakersfield. I've seen it on the map. You go straight there."

"Looks like a very big place on the map," said Ma.

"But if we all lie around here, there's no water and we can't move this car. If you all get out there and start work, you'll all have money and maybe a house to live in. How about it, Casy? Do you want to stay here with me?"

"I'll do whatever you all think," Casy said.

Pa said, "Well, maybe we could do a hundred miles before we stop."

Ma stepped in front of him. "I ain't going."

Pa was surprised at her. "What do you mean? You have to go. You have to look after the family."

Ma went to the back of the car and took a large hammer from the floor. She held it up in her hand and said, "I ain't going to go."

"I tell you, you have to go. We've made up our minds."

"Well, you're going to have to beat me first," she cried, holding the hammer higher in the air.

Ruthie and Winfield laughed. Pa looked helplessly around the group.

"Ma," Tom said. "What's wrong? Have you gone crazy?"

Ma's face softened, but her eyes were still full of anger. "What have we got left in the world? Just us. Just the folks. You want to break up the family."

Tom cried, "Ma, we'll catch up with you. We ain't going to be a long time."

Ma waved the large hammer in the air. "And if we camp and you drive by? Or if we get through—how will we tell you? How will you know who to ask?"

Uncle John said, "But we could be making some money."

The eyes of the whole family moved back to Ma. "The money wouldn't do any good," she said. "We need family."

Tom said calmly, "Ma, we can't camp here. There's no water. And Grandma needs shade."

"All right," she said. "We'll go along. We'll stop at the first place where there's water and shade. And the truck will come back and take you into town to get your part and it will take you back. Then we'll wait for you."

Tom looked at Pa, and then said, "All right, Ma. You win. Now put that thing down before you hurt someone."

Ma looked surprised at the large hammer in her hand. She dropped her weapon on the ground, and Tom carefully picked it up. He said, "Al, you drive the folks on and get them camped, and then you bring the truck back here. Me and the preacher will get that part off."

Al loaded the family back on the truck. Tom had already gone under the car when the family drove off. He said to the preacher, "Casy, you've been quiet these last few days. What's the matter?"

Casy stretched out on his stomach, looking under the car. "I did a lifetime's talking when I was a preacher."

Tom made a few loud noises with the tools. "There it is," he said.

The two men got to their feet and then sat under the shade of a large advertising sign. Casy said, "Tom, I've been watching the cars on the road, those we passed and those that passed us. It's like they're running away from soldiers. It's like the whole country is moving."

"Yeah," Tom said. "The whole country is moving."

"Well, what's going to happen if they can't get jobs out there?"

"Oh, I don't know," Tom cried. "I'm just putting one foot in front of the other. I did that for four years in McAlester."

"Yeah, maybe that's the best way."

"Ain't that Al coming?" Tom asked.

"Yeah. Looks like it."

Tom stood up. The truck arrived. Tom shouted, "What took you so long? Did you have to go far?"

"We had a mess," Al said. "Grandma started crying. Then, Rosasharn started."

"Where did you leave them?" Tom asked.

"Well, we found a camp. It has shade and water. Cost half a dollar to stay there. But Ma says we have to stay there because Grandma's tired. We have the Wilsons' tent up. I think Grandma's going crazy."

Tom looked at the lowering sun. "Casy," he said, "somebody has to stay with this car."

"Sure, I'll stay."

Al took a paper bag from the seat. "Here's some bread and meat Ma sent, and I have a bottle of water here."

Tom got in the truck beside Al and the two drove off. Soon they were at the edge of town, and there on the right was a yard full of old cars, engines rusting on the ground, truck sides, wheels, twisted iron. Al drove the truck up to an old house and Tom got out and looked into the doorway. "Don't see anyone," Tom said. "Anybody here?" he called out.

"I hope they have a '25 Dodge."

Behind the house a door shut and a one-eyed man came out. He was thin and dirty and his jeans and shirt were thick and shiny with oil.

Tom asked, "Are you the boss?"

"I work for the boss." The one eye looked at them. "What do you want?"

"Do you have an old '25 Dodge? We need a part like this," Tom explained, holding the part in his hand.

"I don't know. The boss could tell you, but he went home."

"Can we look and see?"

"Sure, I don't care."

Tom and Al walked among the old cars. The sun disappeared behind the mountains. Al looked around. "Over there, look, Tom! That looks like a '25 or '26."

They walked over to the rusting car, resting on flat tires. "Sure, it's a '25," Al cried. "Can we take a part from it, mister?"

Tom kneeled down and looked under the car. He then slid under it. The one-eyed man said, "I'll get you a box of tools."

Together Tom and Al removed a piece from the engine and got to the part that they needed. There was a bang of metal.

"I got it," Al said. "And I got some rings we could use, too."

Tom stood up and wiped his face and looked at the part. "It looks OK to me. How much will that be, mister?"

The one-eyed man brought out a flashlight and shone it on a book full of the names of parts and their prices. "I don't know exactly. If the boss were here, he'd be able to tell you. How about a dollar?"

"All right," Tom said. "And what will you take for that flashlight?"

"Well, it isn't very good—oh, thirty-five cents."

Tom handed over the silver coins. He and Al got into the truck, and as they drove off Tom shouted, "Bye." The truck went noisily along the road.

Al said, "Tom, did you hear Connie talking about studying at nights. I've been thinking that maybe I'd study at nights, too. Learn about radio or engines. A fellow might get started that way."

"Maybe," Tom said. "There were fellows taking lessons by mail in McAlester. I've never known one of them that finished. They got tired of it."

They fell into silence and the dark came and the stars were sharp and white.

When the truck arrived, Casy got out of the back seat of the car and walked to the side of the road. "I never expected you so soon," he said.

Tom gathered the parts in a sack. "We were lucky," he said. "Got a flashlight, too. We're going to fix it right up."

The men got to work on the car. Casy knelt down and took the flashlight. He kept the beam on the working hands. Tom held the part in place while Al tightened the screws. "I guess that's it," Tom said. They got out from under the car. "OK, Al, try starting it." Al got into the car and stepped on the starter. The motor banged.

Blue smoke poured out of the back. "It'll burn oil like that for a few seconds. It'll be OK. Turn it off now. Let's get some dinner."

"You'd make a good mechanic," Al said to Tom.

"Well, I worked in a shop for a year. We'll drive real slowly for a couple of hundred miles."

Tom and Al quickly ate the boiled pork and drank the water from the bottle. When they finished, Tom said, "All right. I'll drive the car. You bring the truck, Al." The preacher got in the car and Tom started the engine.

There was a small wooden house in the middle of the campground and on the porch of the house a light beamed into a large circle. Half a dozen tents were near the house and cars stood beside the tents. A group of men had gathered on the porch.

Tom drove the car to the side of the road and parked. Al went through the gate in the truck. "No need to take this one in," Tom said. He got out and walked through the gate.

The owner dropped his front chair legs to the floor and leaned forward. "You men want to camp here?"

"No," Tom said. "We have folks here. Hi, Pa."

Pa, seated on the bottom step, said, "Did you get her fixed?"

"We were lucky," Tom said. "Got a part before dark."

"Ma's worried," Pa said. "Your Grandma's gone crazy."

"Yeah, Al told me. Is she any better now?"

"Well, she's sleeping."

The owner said, "If you want to bring the car in and camp, it will cost you fifty cents. You get a place to camp and water and wood."

"What?" said Tom. "We can sleep right beside the road and it won't cost a thing."

The owner said, "But the sheriff comes by at night. He'll make it hard for you. We have a law against sleeping out in this state. We have a law about trespassers."

"If I pay you half a dollar, I'm not a trespasser?" Tom said.

"That's right. Ain't you got half a dollar?"

Tom's eyes stared angrily. "Yeah, but I'm going to need it. I can't use it just for sleeping."

"Well, we all have to make a living," the owner said.

Pa said, "We'll get moving early. Look, mister, we paid. This fellow is a part of our family. Can't he stay? We paid."

"Half a dollar a car," the owner said.

"We'll drive along the road and meet you in the morning," Tom said to Pa. He made a thin cigarette and added, "We'll go along soon."

Pa said to the other men in the circle, "We used to be farmers. Worked all of our lives."

Near the edge of the porch a ragged man stood. His black coat hung in long pieces. He said to Pa, "You folks must have a nice little pot of money."

"No, we don't have any money, now," Pa said. "But there are plenty of us able to work and we're all good men. We'll get good wages out west."

The ragged man stared while Pa spoke, and then he laughed. The circle of faces turned to him. The laughing got out of control and turned into coughing. His eyes became red and watery. "You're going out there?" The laughing started again. He stopped himself. "Picking oranges? Or maybe peaches?"

Pa said, "We're going to take what they have. They have lots of work."

The ragged man said, "Me—I'm coming back. I've been there."

The faces turned quickly toward him. The men became stiff. The ragged man looked at their faces. "I'm going back home to die of hunger. I'd rather die all at once."

Pa said, "What are you talking about? I have a handbill that says there are good wages. And I read that they need folks to pick fruit."

The ragged man turned to Pa. "Do you have any place to go back home?"

"No," said Pa. "We're out. They put a tractor past the house."

"You wouldn't go back then?"

"Of course not."

"Then I'm not going to worry you," said the ragged man. "Handbills? They need men? But you don't know what kind of men they need."

"What are you talking about?"

"Look," said the man. "This fellow wants eight hundred men. So, he prints five thousand of those things and maybe twenty thousand people see them. And maybe two or three thousand folks start moving because of this handbill."

"But it doesn't make any sense!" Pa cried.

"Not until you see the fellow that put out the handbill. You'll see him, or someone who works for him. Maybe he needs two hundred men, so he talks to five hundred, and they tell other folks, and when you get to the place, there are a thousand men. Then the fellow says, 'I'm paying twenty cents an hour.' And maybe half the men walk off. But there are still five hundred that are so hungry they work for bread. Do you see now? If he can get a lot of men, hungry men, he can pay them less." The faces in the circle looked coldly at the man. "Let me tell you. Ask him what he's going to pay. Ask him to write down what he's going to pay."

The owner said, "He's just lying. There's plenty of them going around getting people mad."

The ragged man said, "Well, I tried to tell you folks. I guess you'll have to find out for yourselves." The circle was quiet. The man looked around and then he turned and walked away into the darkness.

Pa said, "Do you think he's telling the truth?"

The preacher answered, "He's telling the truth, all right. The truth for him."

"How about us?" Tom demanded. "Is that the truth for us?"

"I don't know," said Casy.

"I don't know," said Pa.

They walked to the tent and Ma came out to meet them. "All sleeping," she said. "Grandma finally fell asleep." Then she saw Tom. "Is everything all right, Tom?"

"Yeah. We got it fixed," said Tom. "We're ready to go."

"Thank dear God for that," she said.

Pa cleared his throat. "A fellow was just saying . . ."

Tom touched his arm. "Funny what he says," Tom said. "He said that there are lots of folks on the way." Ma looked at them in the darkness. "We'll go now. We'll stop by the road on the right-hand side. Night, Ma."

Chapter 5 The Roadside Camps

The cars of the migrant people came slowly out of the side roads onto the great cross-country highway. In the daylight, they hurried to the west, and as the dark caught them, they grouped near to shelter and water. It might be that one family camped near water, and another camped for the water and some company, and a third because two families found it good. And when the sun came down, maybe twenty families were there. In the evening, a strange thing happened—the twenty families became one family; the children were the children of all.

The Joad family moved slowly up into the mountains of New Mexico. They climbed into the high country of Arizona. There a border guard stopped them. "Where are you going?"

"To California," said Tom.

"How long do you plan to be in Arizona?"

"Long enough to get across."

The guard stuck a sign on the windshield. "OK. Go ahead, but you'd better keep moving."

"Sure. We plan to."

They drove up and down hills, and finally to a great flat area that was all desert. They drove all night and came to the mountains in the night. When the daylight came, they saw the Colorado River below them. They were stopped at the bridge, and a guard washed the sign off their windshield. They crossed the bridge, and finally stopped.

Pa called, "We're here—we're in California!" They looked at the broken rock.

"We've got to the desert," Tom said. "We have to get water and rest."

The Joads and Wilsons drove to the river, and they sat in the cars looking at the beautiful water going by. There was a family camping near the river. Tom leaned his head out of the truck and said, "Can we stop here?"

A heavy woman looked up. "We don't own it, mister. Stop if you want. A cop will be down to have a look at you."

The two cars parked in a clear place on the grass. The tents were passed down, the Wilson tent put up, the Joads' stretched over a rope.

Winfield and Ruthie walked slowly down through the tall grass. Ruthie said, "This is California! And we're right in it." Then the two children walked into the water and stood quietly.

They heard Ma calling, "Ruthie, Winfield! You come back!"

Tom said, "I'm going to go down and take a bath. That's what I'm going to do—before I sleep. How's Grandma since we got her in the tent?"

"Don't know," said Pa. "I couldn't seem to wake her up." A

crying sound came from the tent, and Ma went inside quickly.

"She's woken up," Noah said. "She's out of her senses."

Tom said, "She's exhausted. If she doesn't get some rest soon, she's not going to get there."

He moved away and the other men followed him. They took off their clothes and walked into the water and sat down.

Uncle John put his head under the water for a few seconds. "Well, we're here. This is California."

"We still have to cross the desert," said Tom. "And I hear it's hell."

Noah asked, "Are you going to try tonight?"

"What do you think, Pa?" Tom asked.

"Well, I don't know. It will do us good to get a little rest, especially Grandma. But I'd like to cross it and get settled in a job. Only got about forty dollars left. I'll feel better when we're working and a little money is coming in."

Noah said lazily, "I'd just like to stay here. To lie here forever."

Pa said, "Wait until we get to California. You'll see nice country then."

"Pa, this is California!"

Two men dressed in jeans and blue shirts came through the bushes. "Do you mind if we come in?"

"It ain't our river," Pa said.

The two men shook off their pants and their shirts and stepped out into the water. They were a father and his boy.

Pa asked, "Going west?"

"No. We've just come from there. We're going back home. Can't make a living out there."

Pa asked, "You can't?"

"No. But at least we can die from hunger with folks we know. We won't have a lot of fellows hating us."

Pa said, "What makes them hate you?"

"Don't know," said the man. "You ain't never been in California?"

"No, we ain't."

"Well, don't take my word. Go see for yourself. Yes, it's a nice country. All valleys and fruit. But you can't have any of that. That belongs to a Land and Cattle Company. And if they don't want to work it, it ain't going to get worked. If you go in there and plant a little corn, you'll go to jail!"

"Good land? And they ain't working it?"

"Yes, that's right. And I'll tell you something—they hate you. You haven't been called an 'Oakie' yet."

Tom said, "Oakie? What's that?"

"Well, Oakie used to mean you were from Oklahoma. Now it means you're a dirty nothing. But I can't tell you anything. You have to go there." The man looked at his son and laughed. "You ain't going to get any steady work. You're going to work hard for your dinner. And you're going to do it with people looking mean at you."

Pa asked slowly, "Ain't it nice out there at all?"

"Sure, nice to look at, but you can't have any of it."

The sun was flaming down now. "If a fellow's willing to work hard, can't he make it?" Pa asked.

The man sat up and faced him. "Mister, I don't know everything. You might go out there and fall into a steady job, and I'd be telling lies. And then you might not ever get any work. A fellow doesn't know everything."

Pa turned his head and looked at Uncle John. "What do you think about all of this?"

Uncle John said, "I don't know anything about it. We're going there, ain't we? None of this talk is going to stop us going."

"Yeah," Pa said.

"Well, I'm going over there to get some sleep then."

Tom stood up and walked to the sandy shore. He slipped his clothes on his wet body, walked among the bushes, and lay down. Noah followed him.

"Tom."

"Yeah?"

"Tom, I ain't going on."

Tom sat up. "What do you mean?"

"Tom, I ain't going to leave this water. I'm going to walk on down this river."

"You're crazy," Tom said.

"I'll get a piece of line. I'll catch fish. A fellow can't go hungry beside a nice river."

Tom said, "How about the family? How about Ma?"

"I can't help it. I can't leave this water. You know how it is, Tom. You know how the folks are nice to me. But they don't really care for me."

"You're crazy."

"No, I ain't. I know how I am. I know they're sorry. But, I ain't going. You tell Ma, Tom."

"Now listen to me," Tom began.

"No. I was in that water. And I ain't going to leave it. I'm going now, Tom—down the river. I'll catch fish. I can't leave it. I can't." He stepped out of the bushes. "You tell Ma, Tom." He walked away.

Tom followed him to the river. "Listen, you stupid fool."

"I'm sad. But I can't help it. I have to go." He walked along the shore. Tom started to follow and then he stopped. He watched Noah growing smaller on the edge of the river, until he disappeared from sight. And Tom took off his cap and scratched his head. He went back and lay down to sleep.

In the tent Grandma lay on the bed, and Ma sat beside her, and Rosasharn sat on the other side and watched her mother.

"Told him to come right here," Grandma said. "I'll catch him." She closed her eyes and rolled her head from side to side.

Rosasharn looked helplessly at the old woman. She said softly, "She's awfully sick."

Grandma kicked off the blanket with her legs, which lay like gray, knotted sticks. And then her breathing grew steady and easy, and she slept deeply and breathed through her half-opened mouth. The girl lay down on the edge of the bed and closed her eyes. Ma turned over on her back and crossed her hands under her head. She yawned and then closed her eyes. In her half-sleep, she heard footsteps approaching, but it was a man's voice that awoke her.

"Who's in here?"

Ma sat up quickly. A brown-faced man bent over and looked in. He wore boots and a big silver star was pinned to his shirt at the left breast.

"Who's in here?" he demanded again.

Ma asked, "What do you want, mister?"

"What do you think I want? I want to know who's in here."

"There's just the three of us in here. Me and Grandma and my girl."

"Where are your men?"

"They went down to clean up. We were driving all night."

"Where'd you come from?"

"Oklahoma."

"Well, you can't stay here."

"We plan to get out tonight and cross the desert, mister."

"Well, you'd better. If you're here tomorrow at this time, I'll throw you in jail. We don't want any of you settling down here."

Ma's face was red with anger. "Mister, where I come from you keep your voice down. Frightening women." She came toward him with a cooking pan in her hand. "Go on. I'm glad our men aren't here. They'd pull you to pieces."

The man took two steps backward. "Well, you ain't in your country now. You're in California, and we don't want you Oakies settling down."

"Oakies?" Ma said softly.

"Yeah, Oakies! And if you're here when I come tomorrow, I'll put you in jail." He turned and walked to the next tent and banged on the side with his hand.

Tom heard his name called. "Tom, oh Tom." He sat up and whistled through his teeth. The bushes shook and Ruthie stood looking at him.

"Ma wants you," she said. "Ma wants you right away."

"All right," he said as he stood up. Ruthie ran, and Tom heard her call excitedly for Winfield as she went.

Ma had started a fire and had a pan of water heating. She looked happy when she saw him.

"What's the matter, Ma?" he asked.

"I was scared," she said. "There was a policeman here. He says we can't stay here. I was scared you'd hit him if he talked to you."

"Why would I hit him?"

Ma smiled. "Well, he talked so bad—I nearly hit him myself."

Tom took her arm and he laughed. He sat down on the ground, still laughing. "My God, Ma. I knew you when you were gentle. What's happened to you?"

She looked serious. "I don't know, Tom."

"First you frighten us with that hammer, and now you try to hit a cop." He laughed softly.

"Tom."

"Yeah."

She waited a long time. "Tom, that policeman—he called us Oakies. And he said that we can't stay here."

"Did he say why?"

"He said that we ain't at home now. We're in California."

Tom said slowly, "Ma, I have something to tell you. Noah—he went on down the river. He ain't going on."

It took a moment for Ma to understand. "Why?" she asked softly.

"I don't know. He said that he has to."

"How will he eat?"

"I don't know. He said he'll catch fish."

Ma was silent for a long time. "The family's falling apart," she said. "I don't know. Seems like I can't think. I just can't think. There's too much happening."

Tom said, "He'll be all right, Ma. He's a funny kind of guy."

The other men came up from the river. Their eyes were full of sleep. Pa said, "What's the matter?"

"We're going," said Tom. "A cop said we have to go. We can get a good start. It's nearly three hundred miles where we're going."

Pa said, "I thought we were going to rest."

"Well, we ain't. We have to go, Pa," Tom said. "Noah ain't going. He walked on down the river."

"Ain't going? What's the matter with him?"

"Well, we have to go," said Tom.

Wilson walked near for the last words. "We can't go, folks," he said. "Sairy can't go. If they jail us, well, they jail us. She's got to rest and get strong."

Pa said, "Maybe we can wait and go together."

"No," Wilson said. "You've been nice to us, but you can't stay here. You have to get on and get jobs. We ain't going to let you stay."

Pa said excitedly, "But you ain't got anything."

Wilson smiled and said, "We never had anything. Now you go, or I'll get mean and mad."

The men started loading up the truck, Uncle John on top,

while the others passed things up to him. Tom said, "With the load we're taking, this old wagon will boil her head off. We have to have plenty of water."

Ma passed the boiled potatoes out. The family ate standing, throwing the hot potatoes from hand to hand until they cooled. Then, the men went into the tent. Grandma was still asleep, her mouth wide open. They lifted the whole bed and gently passed it up to the top of the truck. Grandma moved her head, but she did not wake.

Ma went into the Wilsons' tent for about ten minutes and came out quietly. "It's time to go," she said.

The family climbed on the truck, Ma on top, beside Grandma. Tom and Al and Pa sat in the seat, and Winfield on Pa's knees. Connie and Rosasharn made a nest against the front. The preacher, Uncle John, and Ruthie were close together on the load.

Pa called, "Goodbye." There was no answer from the Wilsons' tent. Tom started the engine and the truck slowly moved away. Tom drove into a gas station and checked the tires for air. He had the truck filled with gas and bought two five-gallon cans of gas and a two-gallon can of oil. He looked at a map.

The gas station boy in his white uniform seemed anxious until the bill was paid. "You people sure have courage. Crossing in this old truck."

The truck was back on the road and moved on over the hot earth, and the hours passed. Ruthie and Winfield went to sleep. Connie loosened a blanket from the load and covered himself and Rosasharn with it.

On the back of the truck Ma lay on the bed beside Grandma and she could not see with her eyes but she could feel the struggling body and the struggling heart. And Ma said, "All right. It's going to be all right. You know the family has to get across. You know that."

It was near midnight when they came to the next inspection station. A guard came out from an office and wrote down the license number and looked around. Tom asked, "What's this about?"

"Inspection. We have to look over your stuff. Do you have any vegetables or seeds?"

"No," said Tom.

"Well, we have to look over your stuff. You have to unload."

Ma climbed down from the truck. "Look, mister. We have a sick old lady. We have to get her to a doctor. We can't wait. You can't make us wait."

"Yeah? Well, we have to look you over."

"I swear we ain't got anything," Ma cried. "I swear. And Grandma's really sick." Ma pulled herself up to the back of the truck. "Look," she said.

The guard shot a flashlight up on the old thin face. "By God, she is," he said. "Do you swear you don't have any seeds or fruits or vegetables, no corn, no oranges?"

"No, no. We don't!"

"Then go ahead. You can get a doctor in Barstow. That's only eight miles. Go on ahead."

Tom climbed in and drove on. He increased the speed, and in the little town of Barstow he stopped, got out, and walked around to the back of the truck. Ma leaned out, "It's all right. Let's not stop here. We need to get across."

"But how's Grandma?"

"She's all right. Drive on. We have to get across."

They drove through the night. In the morning light, the sun came up behind them, and then—suddenly, they saw the great valley below them. Al stepped on the brake and stopped in the middle of the road. "Wow! Look!" he said. The rows of fruit trees, the great flat valley, green and beautiful, and the farmhouses.

Pa said, "God!"

Al drove to the side of the road and parked. "I just want to look at it." The grain fields golden in the morning.

Pa said, "I never knew there was anything like this." The peach trees and the dark green areas of oranges. And the red roofs of barns among the trees. Al got out.

He called, "Ma—come look. We're there!"

Ruthie and Winfield hurried down from the car, and then they stood, silent before the great valley. Ruthie whispered, "It's California."

Winfield said, "There's fruit."

Casy and Uncle John, Connie and Rosasharn climbed down. And they stood silently.

Tom said, "Where's Ma? I want Ma to see it. Look, Ma!" Ma was climbing out slowly and stiffly. Tom looked at her. "Ma, are you sick?"

Her voice was weak. "Did you say we crossed?"

Tom pointed to the great valley. "Look!"

She turned her head and her mouth opened a little. "Thank God!" she said. "The family's here."

"Are you sick, Ma?"

"No, just tired."

"Didn't you get any sleep?"

"No."

"Was Grandma bad?"

Ma raised her eyes and looked over the valley. "Grandma's dead."

They looked at her, all of them, and Pa asked, "When?"

"Before they stopped us last night."

"So that's why you didn't want them to look."

"I was afraid we wouldn't get across," she said. "I told Grandma that we couldn't help her. The family had to get across. I told her."

Tom said, "Wow. You were lying there with her all night long!"

"The family had to get across."

"We have to go now," Pa said. "We have to go on down."

Al climbed on the load to make room for Ma in the seat. He sat down beside Casy and Uncle John. "Well, she was old."

Tom and Ma and Pa got into the front seat. The sun was behind them and the valley, gold and green, was in front of them. Ma said, "It's pretty. It's a pity that Grandpa and Grandma ain't here to see this."

"Yeah, it's a pity," Pa said.

And the truck rolled down the mountain into the great valley.

Chapter 6 Hoovervilles

In Kansas and Arkansas, in Oklahoma and Texas and New Mexico, the tractors moved in and pushed the tenants out. Three hundred thousand in California and more coming. And in California there was a Hooverville on the edge of every town. The tiny town lay close to the water and the houses were tents and large boxes, a great trash pile.

The family, on top of the load, the children and Connie and Rosasharn and the preacher, were stiff and uncomfortable. They had sat in the heat in front of the coroner's office in Bakersfield while Pa and Ma and Uncle John went in. Al and Tom walked along the street and looked into the store windows. Then a basket was brought out and Grandma was lifted down from the truck.

At last Pa and Ma and Uncle John came out, and they were quiet. Pa looked at Ma and said, "There wasn't anything else we could do. We didn't have enough money."

"I know," Ma said. "But she always wanted a nice funeral."

"Where are we going?" Tom asked.

Pa raised his hat and scratched his head. "Camp," he said. "We ain't going to spend our last few dollars until we get work. Drive out in the country."

Tom started the car and they rolled through the streets and out toward the country. And by a bridge they saw a group of tents and large boxes. Tom said, "Why don't we stop here? We can find out where work is." He drove down to the edge of the camp.

There was no order in the camp. Little gray tents, houses made of boxes and rusted metal. A group of boxes lay about, boxes to sit on, to eat on. Tom stopped the truck and looked at Pa. "It ain't pretty," he said. "Do you want to go someplace else?"

Pa said, "We have to ask about work." Tom opened the door and stepped out, as the family climbed down from the load and looked curiously at the camp. A young man was working on an old car. He looked over at the Joad's truck. Pa said, "Could we camp here?"

"Sure, why not. Have you folks just come across?"

"Yeah," said Tom. "We just got in this morning."

"Have you never been in Hooverville before?"

"Where's Hooverville?"

"This is it."

"Oh!" said Tom. "We just got in."

Ma said, "Let's get the camp up. I'm tired. Maybe we can all rest." Pa and Uncle John climbed up on the truck to unload the tent and the bed.

The young man said to Tom, "But you can't stay too long. If you just stay in one camp, you'll see how quick a sheriff will push you along."

"But what for?"

"I don't know. Some people say that they don't want us to vote. Keep us moving so we can't vote. And some say that if we settled in one place, we'd get organized."

"We're looking for work," Tom told him. "We'll take any kind of work. Back home some fellows came through with handbills—orange ones. It said they need lots of people out here to work the crops."

The young man laughed. "They say that there are three hundred thousand of us here, and I bet every family has seen those handbills."

"But there is work," Tom said. "With all of the stuff that's growing around here—vegetables, grapes—I've seen it. They have to have men." A baby cried from inside a tent, and the young man walked away, shaking his head.

Inside the Joad tent, Connie and Rosasharn were talking quietly. Connie's eyes were watery. "If I'd known that it was going to be like this, I wouldn't have come. I would have studied nights about tractors back home and got a three-dollar job. A fellow can live well on three dollars a day, and go to the picture show every night, too."

Rosasharn looked worried. "You're going to study nights about radios," she said. He was silent. "Ain't you?" she demanded.

"Yeah, sure. As soon as I get a little money."

She rolled up on her elbow. "You ain't giving it up!"

"No, no—of course not. But—I didn't know there were places like this that we'd have to live in."

The girl's eyes hardened. "You have to," she said.

Ma knelt beside the fire, breaking sticks to keep the flames up under the pot of soup. The children of the camp, fifteen of them, stood and watched. "How long have you been in California?" Ma asked an older girl.

"Oh, about six months. We lived in a government camp for a short time, and then we went north, and when we came back it was full. That was a nice place to live."

"Where's that?" Ma asked.

"Over by Weedpatch. Got nice toilets and bathtubs, and you can wash clothes in a tub, and at night the folks play music and on Saturday nights they have a dance."

Ma said, "I'd like to go there."

Al had walked along to where the young man was working on his car. "Can I help you with that?" he asked.

"Well, yeah, I could use some help," the young man said. "My name's Floyd Knowles."

"I'm Al Joad." He took out his pocketknife. "There isn't anything I love more than the inside of an engine."

Floyd then said, "You know, I've been here for six months. Going all over this state, trying to find work."

"Ain't there any work?" Al asked.

"No, there ain't any steady work."

The two young men continued to work and talk about jobs.

"Al!" Winfield called out. "Al, dinner's ready."

Al wiped his hands on his pants. "We ain't eaten today," he said to Floyd. "I'll come back and help after I've eaten."

Ma mixed the soup more and put some in bowls for the family. After dinner, Al said to Tom, "Come with me."

They walked away together. "What's the matter with you?" Tom asked.

"Just wait." He led Tom to the broken car. "This is Floyd Knowles," he said.

"Yeah, I talked to him before. How are you?"

"Just getting this old thing repaired," Floyd said.

"Floyd just told me. Tell him, Floyd."

Floyd said, "A fellow came through and he said there's going to be work up north."

"Up north?"

"Yeah."

"What kind of work?"

"Picking fruit. It's near ready."

"How far?" Tom demanded.

"Oh, about two hundred miles."

"That's a long way," Tom said. "How do we know there's going to be work when we get there?"

"Well, we don't know," said Floyd. "But there ain't anything here. This fellow got a letter from his brother about it. And he said don't tell anybody, or there'll be too many. We need to get out at night."

Tom said, "Well, I don't know. It's just a long way. And we hoped we could get work here and rent a house to live in."

Floyd said patiently, "I know you just got here. There's stuff you have to learn. You ain't going to settle down because there ain't work to settle you."

A bright new car turned off the highway and headed down into the camp. It pulled into the center of the camp. "Who's this?" Tom asked Floyd.

"I don't know—cops maybe."

The car door opened and a man got out and stood beside the car. Inside the car another man remained seated. The first man said, "Do you men want to work? A place called Tulare. Fruit's ready. We need a lot of pickers."

Floyd spoke up, "Are you doing the hiring?"

"Well, I'm contracting the land."

The men of the camp all grouped around now. One of the men asked, "What are you paying?"

"Well, I don't know exactly. About thirty cents."

"Why don't you know?"

"Well, it depends on the price of fruit."

Floyd stepped ahead. He said quietly, "I'll go, mister. You just need to give us a written order for work, showing us where and how much and we'll sign it."

The contractor said angrily, "Are you telling me how to do my job?" He turned to the new car and said, "Joe!"

The man in the car stepped out. He was wearing tall boots and a brown uniform and a sheriff's star on his shirt. "What do you want?"

"Have you ever seen this man, Joe?" The contractor asked, pointing to Floyd.

"What did he do?"

"He was talking and causing trouble."

"Hmm." The sheriff moved around Floyd slowly.

"You see!" Floyd cried. "If this guy was honest, he wouldn't need a cop with him."

"Yeah, maybe I have seen him before," the sheriff said. "He looks like one of the guys wanted for stealing a car just last week." He shouted at Floyd, "Get in the car!"

"You have nothing against him," Tom said.

The sheriff said to Tom, "If I were you, I'd keep my mouth shut."

The contractor turned back to the men. "Don't listen to these troublemakers—they'll get you in trouble. I can use all of you in Tulare."

The men did not answer.

The sheriff turned back to them. "Maybe we should go," he said. He had a thin smile on his face. "The Health Department says that we have to clean out this camp. You fellows should go to Tulare. That's just a friendly way of telling you. A bunch of men might be here later. Someone might get hurt if you ain't gone."

"That's all," the contractor said. "Men needed in Tulare."

"Yeah, that's all. I don't want to see you here tomorrow morning." The sheriff then looked at Floyd. "Now you get in that car."

Floyd looked at Tom, then he swung around and hit the sheriff hard in the face, and then he was away, running past the tents. The sheriff started to fall back but then moved forward and Tom put out his foot. The sheriff fell over it and rolled, reaching for his gun. But Floyd was out of sight. The sheriff fired from the ground. A woman screamed and then looked at her bloody hand. The sheriff raised his gun again. The men in the group gathered around him and Casy stepped up and kicked him in the neck. The sheriff became unconscious. The motor of the new car sounded loudly as the car drove off.

A crowd gathered around the woman with the broken hand. Casy moved close to Tom. "You have to get out," he said. "Go down by the river and hide. He saw you put your foot out."

"I don't want to go," said Tom.

Casy whispered, "They'll fingerprint you. You broke parole. They'll send you back."

"Oh! I forgot!"

"Go quick," Casy said. "Before he gets up." Then he turned to Al. "Get out," he said. "Go on, get out—to the tent. You don't know anything."

"Yeah? How about you?"

Casy smiled at him. "Somebody has to take the blame. And your ma and pa will get in trouble and they'll send Tom back to McAlester."

Al considered it for a moment. "OK," he said. "I think you're a fool, though."

Tires screamed on the highway and an open car came quickly into the camp. Four men with guns got out. Casy walked to them.

"What's going on here?"

Casy said, "I knocked out your man there."

One of the men with guns went to the sheriff. He was conscious. "What happened here?"

"Well," said Casy, "he got mean, so I hit him. And then he

started shooting—hit a woman over there. So I hit him again."

"What did you do in the first place?"

"I talked back," said Casy.

"Get in the car."

The sheriff was up. He looked at Casy. "It doesn't look like him."

"It was me," Casy said. "You got smart with the wrong fellow."

When the police had gone, the people came out of the tents. The sun was down now and a gentle blue evening light was in the camp. The women went back to the fires and the men came together to talk softly.

Rosasharn moved weakly out of the tent. "Where's Connie?" she asked angrily. "I ain't seen Connie for a long time. Where did he go?"

"I ain't seen him," Ma said.

The tears started again in Rosasharn's eyes. She went back toward the tent. The girl knelt down and started preparing the potatoes. She said, "Wait until I see him. I'll tell him."

Uncle John dug with his thumb into a small pocket of his blue jeans and took out a dirty folded bill. He spread it out and showed it to Pa. "Five dollars," he said.

"Steal it?" Pa asked.

"No, I had it. Kept it to get drunk. I knew there was going to be a time when I would have to get drunk. The preacher went and gave himself up to save Tom. I just have to get drunk."

Pa took the dirty bill and gave Uncle John two dollars. "There you are," he said. "A fellow has to do what he has to do."

Uncle John stood up and walked away. Pa and Ma and the children watched him walk up to the highway and across the road to the grocery store.

Ruthie whispered to Winfield, "I'm going to get drunk." She

swung around and crossed her eyes and let her tongue hang out. "Look at me. I'm drunk."

"Look," Winfield cried. "I'm Uncle John." He spun around and then fell to the ground.

Al and Tom walked quietly toward the camp, and they saw the children walking strangely. Tom stopped and said, "Are you two crazy?"

The children stopped—embarrassed. "We were just playing," Ruthie said.

"It's a crazy way to play," Tom said.

Ruthie said, "It ain't any crazier than a lot of things."

Tom and Al continued to walk quietly. Tom said, "Why did Casy do that? He'd been talking about how he hadn't done anything for us. He's a funny fellow, Al. Thinking all the time."

They walked past the tents. Floyd popped his head out of his tent. "Are you getting out?"

Tom said, "I don't know. Do you think we should?"

Floyd laughed. "They'll burn you out if you don't. One of their men took a beating tonight. Yeah, they'll burn us out."

Al said, "A fellow told me about a government camp near here. Where is it?"

"Oh, I think that's full."

"Well, where is it?"

"Go south on highway 99 about fourteen miles, and turn east to Weedpatch. But I think it's full."

"A fellow says it's nice," Al said.

"We have to move on," Tom said. "Bye, Floyd."

"Bye," Floyd said. "Hope to see you again."

The frying pan of potatoes was cooking over the fire. Ma moved the thick slices around with a spoon. Pa and Rosasharn sat near the fire.

"It's Tom!" Ma cried. "Thank God."

"We have to get out of here," said Tom. "They're going to burn the camp down tonight."

Rosasharn demanded, "Have you seen Connie?"

"Yeah," said Al. "Going south, up the river."

"Was he going away?"

"I don't know."

Ma turned to the girl. "Rosasharn, you've been talking and acting strangely. What did Connie say to you?"

Rosasharn said sadly, "He said that he was sorry he hadn't stayed home and studied about tractors."

They were all quiet. Then Pa said, "Connie wasn't any good. I saw that a long time ago."

Rosasharn got up and went into the tent.

"Sh," Ma said to Pa.

"Well, he ain't any good," repeated Pa. "All the time saying what he's going to do, then doing nothing."

"Sh!" Ma said softly.

Tom interrupted, "Hey. We're not sure Connie's gone forever. We don't have time for talking. We have to eat and get on our way."

Ma had been turning the potatoes in the hot oil. Now she made her decision. "Come on!" she cried. "Let's eat. We have to go quick."

Pa said, "How about John?"

"Where is Uncle John?" Tom asked.

Pa and Ma were silent for a moment and then Pa said, "He went to get drunk."

"What?" Tom said. "Where did he go?"

"I don't know," said Pa.

Tom stood up. "Look," he said, "you eat and get the stuff loaded. I'll go look for Uncle John." Tom walked away quickly. He went across the road to the grocery store. When he walked inside, he saw a gray man behind the counter. "Good evening," he said.

"Good evening," said the man. "Are you looking for something?"

"My uncle," Tom said.

The gray man looked puzzled and worried at the same time. "Ten times a day someone comes in here looking for someone."

"Well, did you see a fellow about sixty years old, wearing black pants, buying alcohol?"

"Well, yes I did," said the man. "I've never seen so much drinking, so I looked after him. He went down to the river. Six cans of the strong stuff. He won't be far away."

Tom said, "Thank you, mister. Oh, and if you see a young man named Connie, tell him we went south." He went outside and crossed the highway and walked along the edge of it. Below him in the sunken field lay the Hooverville. Tom stopped and listened. A voice sang out.

The dull voice sang, "I've given my heart to Jesus, so Jesus take me home." Tom followed the voice down to the river. He saw Uncle John holding an empty bottle and moving his body from side to side.

Tom said quietly, "Hey, Uncle John."

Uncle John turned his head. "Who are you?"

"You forgot me already?"

"No, Tom. Don't try to trick me. I'm all alone here."

"Listen to me, Uncle John. We're going to move on. You come along and you can sleep on the load."

John shook his head. "No. Go on. I ain't going. I'm going to stay here."

"Come on now, Uncle John," Tom said.

Uncle John just shook his head. Tom bent down close to Uncle John and hit him on the chin. Uncle John's head fell back and then forward with the rest of his body. Tom stood up and lifted the body over his shoulders.

When Tom returned to the camp, the truck was loaded and ready. Tom and Al pushed Uncle John onto the load.

"All ready," said Pa.

Tom asked, "Where's Rosasharn?"

"Over there," said Ma. "Come on, Rosasharn. We're going now."

The girl sat with her head bent down. "I ain't going." She did not raise her head.

"You have to go."

"I want Connie. I ain't going until he comes back."

Three cars pulled out of the camp, up the road to the highway, old cars loaded with tents and people.

Tom said, "Connie will find us. I left a message at the store. He'll find us."

Ma said, "Come on, honey."

"I want to wait."

"He'll find us," Tom said. "Don't worry."

Rosasharn and Ma walked slowly together to the truck. Pa and Al and Tom got into the seat. When everyone else was on the load, Tom drove off.

The truck climbed up to the highway. Behind them, a little row of red lights that looked like flames ran across the highway toward the Hooverville. Tom stopped the truck at the side of the road. He watched the red lights cross the entrance of the dirt road and continue on. In a few moments, there came the sounds of shouts and screams and then flames rose from the direction of the camp. Tom turned on the engine and turned the car south.

Ma asked carefully, "Where are we going, Tom?"

"I'm going to look for that government camp," Tom said. "A fellow said that they don't have any cops there."

Chapter 7 The Government Camp

The migrants would work for low wages. They would work for food. And this was good because wages went down and prices stayed up. The landowners were glad and they sent out more handbills to bring more people in. And now the great owners and companies bought the little farms.

It was late when Tom Joad drove along a country road looking for the Weedpatch camp. There were few lights in the countryside. Ma had been sleeping in the seat and Pa had been quiet for a long time. Tom saw a sign and then stopped. A high wire fence faced the road. Tom got out and asked the guard, "Do you have any room here for us?"

"I have one place left. Drive down to the end of that line. You'll be in Unit Four." Tom drove slowly down the long dark row of tents. "Park here," the guard said.

Al jumped off the truck and walked around. Tom said, "You and Pa unload while I go to the office."

Tom followed the guard through the dark to the office. The guard sat down at a desk and took out a form. While Tom filled in the form, the guard explained, "The camp costs a dollar a week but you can work instead, carrying garbage, keeping the camp clean—stuff like that."

"We'll work," Tom said.

"You'll see the committee tomorrow. They'll show you how to use the camp and tell you the rules."

Tom said, "What committee is this?"

The guard sat back in his chair. "It works pretty nice. There are five units. Each unit elects a central committee and that committee makes the laws."

"Do you mean there ain't any cops?"

"No cops. No cop can come in here without a reason. Now you go get some sleep."

"Good night," said Tom.

"Good night," said the guard.

Tom returned to the truck and climbed into the back. He lay down on his back on the wooden floor. The night grew cooler. Tom buttoned his coat over his chest. The stars were clear and sharp over his head.

It was dark when he awoke. The sound of a cooking pan scratching across a stove woke him. Tom looked down the line of tents and saw a small orange light outside one of them. Then, he saw a girl working around the stove. He climbed out of the truck and moved closer. He smelled frying bacon and baking-bread.

"Good morning," she said and turned the bacon in the pan. Then, two men appeared.

"Morning," said the older man.

"Good morning," said Tom.

And then the younger man said, "Morning."

Now the older man said to Tom, "Have you had any breakfast yet?"

"Well, no, I ain't. But my folks are over there. They ain't up. Need the sleep."

"Well, sit down with us. We have plenty—thank God."

"Thank you," said Tom. "It smells so good I can't say no."

They had all started eating when the younger man said, "We're laying some pipe. If you want to walk over with us, maybe we can get you some work."

Tom said, "Well, that's very nice of you. And thank you for the breakfast." After they finished eating, the men got up and Tom said, "Just wait a minute. I have to go tell my folks."

Tom hurried back to the Joad tent. Ruthie was awake and looking around outside. He moved up to her and said, "Listen. Don't wake anybody up, but when they get up, tell them I have a chance at a job. And tell Ma I ate breakfast with the neighbors."

Ruthie agreed and turned her head away. She then walked toward a large building with an open door.

The camp had begun to come to life. At the new fires the women worked, slicing meat, making the bread. And the men were moving around the tents and the cars. The sun showed its edge over the mountains.

Tom went back to the neighbors and said, "It seems funny. I've eaten your food, and I ain't told you my name—I'm Tom Joad."

The older man said, "Well, I'm Timothy Wallace, and this is my boy, Wilkie."

Tom said, "Have you been here long?"

"Ten months," Wilkie said.

"We're working for a Mr. Thomas," Timothy said. "Nice job."

Tom asked, "Don't you have a car?"

Both Wallaces were silent, and Tom saw that they were embarrassed.

Timothy said, "No, we don't have a car. We sold our car. Had to, for food. Couldn't get a job."

They turned off the highway and walked down a small road. Behind some trees they came to a small white farmhouse. As the three men walked past the house, a door banged shut and a heavy sunburned man came down the back steps.

"Morning, Mr. Thomas," Timothy said.

"Good morning." The man spoke angrily.

Timothy said, "This is Tom Joad. We wondered if you need another pair of hands?"

Thomas looked hard at Tom and then laughed. "Oh, sure! I'll take him. I'll take everybody. Maybe I'll take a hundred men."

"We just thought—" Timothy said, apologizing.

Mr. Thomas stopped him. "Yes, I've been thinking, too." He turned around to face them. "I've been paying you thirty cents an hour, right?"

"Yes, Mr. Thomas."

"Well, this morning you're getting twenty-five cents an hour, and you can take it or leave it." His face became red with anger.

Timothy said, "We've given you good work. You said so yourself."

"I know. But it seems like I'm not hiring my own men now," he said. "Did you ever hear of the Farmers' Association?"

"Sure."

"Well, I belong to it. We had a meeting last night. Now, do you know who runs the Farmers' Association? I'll tell you. The Bank of the West. That bank owns most of this valley. A person from the bank told me, 'You're paying thirty cents an hour. You need to cut it down to twenty-five. The wage is now twenty-five. If you pay thirty, it'll cause problems.' And, he said to me, 'You're going to need to borrow money for another crop next year.'" Mr. Thomas stopped. His breathing was heavy. "You see, I have no choice."

Timothy shook his head. "I don't know what to say."

"Now, are you going to work? Twenty-five cents?"

Timothy looked at the ground. "I'll work."

"Me too," said Wilkie.

Tom said, "It seems like I walked into something. Sure, I'll work. I have to."

Mr. Thomas wiped his mouth and chin. "I don't know how long this can go on. I don't know how you men can feed a family on what you get." He looked at his watch. "Well, I'm going to tell you something. You fellows live in the government camp, don't you?"

Timothy said, "Yes."

"And you have dances every Saturday night?"

Wilkie smiled. "We sure do."

Mr. Thomas looked worried. "Don't tell anyone that I told you. The Association doesn't like the government camps. They can't get cops in there. But if there was a big fight and maybe shooting, then they could send cops in. Don't you ever tell where you heard this. But there's going to be a fight this Saturday night and the cops will be ready to go in."

Tom demanded, "Why? Those folks aren't bothering anybody."

"Go on to work," Mr. Thomas said. "And it's twenty-five cents an hour." He walked toward the house.

The three men walked out past the little barn and along a field. They came to a long narrow hole with pieces of pipe lying beside it. They picked up shovels and began to work.

Ruthie walked carefully into the entrance of the Joad tent and looked inside. Winfield saw her and got out from under the blanket. Ma and Pa and the others were still asleep. "Come on," Ruthie whispered.

They went into the large building. The toilets were lined up on one side of the room. "There," said Ruthie. "Those are toilets. I've seen them in a magazine." The children went near to one of the toilets. Winfield was embarrassed. His hand twisted the lever. There was a loud sound as the water ran into the toilet. The children jumped into the air and stepped away. The sound of running water continued. "You broke it," Ruthie said.

"Did not." The two children hurried back to the tent.

The sun was coming up just over the mountain and the camp was waking up. The fires were burning in camp stoves. The smell of smoke was in the air.

Ma stood outside the tent. She saw the children and came over to them. "I was worried," Ma said. "I didn't know where you were."

"We were just looking," Ruthie said.

"Well, where's Tom? Have you seen him?"

Ruthie became important. "Yes, Ma. He said to tell you he got work."

Ma looked back into the tent. "Pa," she called excitedly. "John, get up! You, Al, get up and get washed. All of you, get up and get washed. Tom's gone out and got some work. Now get up!"

Rosasharn said sadly, "I don't feel good. I want Connie."

A frying pan smoked over the fire. The smell of coffee began to fill the air. Pa wandered back from the wash tubs. He said, "Did you say that Tom's got work?"

"Yes. He went out before we woke up," Ma said.

After they ate, Al got in the truck. "I have to get gas," he said. He started the engine. Pa and Uncle John climbed in beside him and the truck moved away down the street.

Rosasharn came over to Ma. "They have hot and cold water and the water comes flooding down," the girl said.

"Well, I'm going to have a bath after I finish here," Ma said.

"I'm going to have one every day," Rosasharn said. "There was a lady in there, too. And she said that there's a nurse who comes every week. The nurse will tell me what to do so the baby's strong."

Ma said, "Praise God."

The truck moved along the beautiful roads, past lines of peach trees that were beginning to color. At each entrance gate Al slowed and at each gate there was a sign: *No Help Wanted. No Trespassing.*

Then Al said, "How are you feeling, Uncle John?"

"I ache," said Uncle John. "I ache all over and I deserve it. I ought to go away where I don't bring problems to my own folks."

Pa put his hand on John's knee. "Listen," he said, "don't you go running away. We're losing folks all the time—Grandpa and Grandma dead—Noah and Connie gone—and the preacher in jail." They drove back to the camp in silence.

Ma got up when she saw Pa coming down the street. He came near and she said, "Did you get any work?"

"No," he said ashamed. "We looked."

Ma said sadly, "This is a nice place. We could be happy here."

"If we got some work."

She looked at him and she closed her eyes slowly.

Pa said, "I saw some birds today heading south."

Ma smiled. "Remember?" she said. "Remember what we always said at home. Winter's coming early when the birds fly." She looked gently at Pa. "I think about home too. I want to forget it. And Noah."

The next day was Saturday. Wilkie went over to another young man and said, "Have you heard about tonight?"

The young man smiled, "Yeah!"

"What have you done?" Wilkie asked.

"Well, I have twenty more men—all good strong boys. They're going to dance and keep their eyes open and their ears open. And at the first sign of any talk or argument, they'll close in tight. When they move out, the fellows will go out with them."

"Tell them they mustn't hurt the fellows."

And now the evening darkness was falling and the practicing of the string band seemed to grow louder. Around the camp, the guards sat in the grass and waited. The cars of guests began to arrive, small farmers and their families, migrants from other camps. And as each guest came through the gate, he mentioned the name of the camper who invited him.

Pa and Uncle John were sitting with a group of men by the office. "We nearly got work today," Pa said. "We were just a few minutes late."

Tom stood at the gate and watched people coming into the dance. Jule, half Cherokee Indian, stood next to Tom. Then three young men came through the gate—young working men in jeans. "I think those are our fellows," Jule said.

"How do you know?"

"I don't know. I just feel it," Jule said.

The dancing started. Boys and girls, men and women moved around creating large squares on a large platform. Ma and Rosasharn sat and watched around the platform with some of the old folks and children. The three young men walked onto the platform and one said, "I'll dance with this girl here."

A blond boy looked up in surprise. "She's my partner."

"Listen, you little fool."

Off in the darkness, a whistle sounded. The three were walled in now. And each one felt hands tightly on their wrists. And then the wall of men moved slowly off the platform.

A large car drove to the entrance. The driver called, "Open up. We hear you have a fight."

The guard did not move. "We don't have a fight here. Listen to that music. Who are you?"

"Police. Open up."

"Got a reason?"

"We don't need one if there's a fight here."

"Well, there's no fight here," said the guard.

The men in the car listened to the music and then moved slowly away and parked across the road and waited.

Chapter 8 Migrant Work

The companies and banks that owned the large farms also owned the factories that canned the fruit. They paid the pickers low wages and made the price of fresh fruit go down. The little farmers watched debt come up on them like the tide. They could not pay wages for pickers and they could not pick the crop. The fruit was burned. A million people hungry, needing the fruit, and the fruit was burned.

In the Weedpatch camp, on a quiet evening, the Joad family sat around after supper. "We have to do something," Ma said. "One month we've been here. And Tom had five days of work. And the rest of you looking every day and no work."

They looked at the ground. "We have to go," Pa said. "We don't want to go. It's nice here. The folks are nice. We don't want to live in one of those Hoovervilles."

"But if we have to, we have to," Ma said. "We have to eat."

Uncle John said, "A fellow said that there's cotton near Tulare. It's not very far, the fellow said."

"Well, we have to go quick. I ain't staying here, though it's nice." Ma picked up her bucket and walked toward the water pipe. She returned with a bucket of hot water. "We'll go in the morning." She looked at Rosasharn. "Are you feeling all right?"

"I ain't had the milk the nurse said I should have," the girl said softly.

"I know. We just don't have any milk."

Rosasharn said sadly, "If Connie hadn't gone away, we would have had a little house by now, with him studying. I'd have the milk I need. I'd have a nice baby."

"We'll get you some milk soon."

It was still dark when Ma woke up her camp. "Come on, get up. We have to get on our way." She slipped on her dress over the underclothes she wore to bed. "We don't have any coffee," she said. "I have a few pieces of bread. We can eat them on the road. Just get up now and we'll load the truck. Don't make any noise. Don't want to wake up the neighbors."

The family dressed. The men pulled down the tent and loaded up the truck. "All right, Ma," Tom said. "We're ready."

Ma held the pieces of bread in her hand. "Now just one each. That's all we have."

Ruthie and Winfield took their bread and climbed into the truck and covered themselves with a blanket and fell asleep again. Tom got into the driver's seat and started the engine.

The light morning traffic moved speedily by on the highway, and the sun grew warm and bright. The family stopped to fix a flat tire. Tom was pumping the tire when a small truck stopped beside them.

A man dressed in a gray business suit got out and walked over to Tom. "Good morning," he said pleasantly.

Tom stopped pumping and looked up. "Good morning."

The man ran his fingers through his graying hair. "Are you people looking for work?"

"We sure are, mister."

"Well, there's plenty of work for you about forty miles north, picking peaches."

"If you tell us how to get there, we'll go now," Tom said.

"Well, you go north to Pixley, that's thirty-five miles. Then you turn east and go for about six miles. Ask anybody where the Hooper Ranch is."

"Thank you, mister," said Tom. The man tipped his hat and drove off. Tom and Al threw the tools into the car. "Come on, let's go," Tom called. "We're going to get some work at last."

They drove through the sunny morning fields. Ma said excitedly, "With four men working, we can buy coffee, and meat, and milk. The nurse said Rosasharn needs milk."

Al said, "I'm going to save some money and then I'm going into a town and getting a job at a garage. I'll live in a nice room and eat at restaurants."

As they came near to the Hooper Ranch, the road was suddenly blocked with cars. A line of white motorcycles was parked along the roadside. "It looks like an accident," Tom said.

A policeman came walking down the road and held up his hand and Al stopped the truck. The policeman leaned on the side of the car. "Where are you going?" he asked.

Al said, "A fellow said that there was work here picking peaches."

"Want to work, do you?"

"Sure do," said Tom.

"OK. Wait here a minute." He moved to the side of the road and called, "One more. That's six cars ready. We'd better take them through."

Then a group of motorcycles came toward the line of six cars. The Joad truck was directed to the back of the line. Two motorcycles led the way and two followed at the back. Tom said anxiously, "I wonder what's wrong."

"Maybe the road's closed," Al suggested.

"They don't need four cops to lead us. I don't like it."

Suddenly, the leading policeman turned off the road into a wide entrance. The old cars followed. Tom saw a line of men along the side of the road, screaming and shaking their fists. When they were away from the entrance, the six cars were told to stop. Two men with large notebooks went from car to car. "Do you want to work?"

"Sure," Tom said. "But, what is this?"

"It's not your business. Do you want to work?"

"Sure we do."

"OK. Find house number sixty-three. Wages are five cents a box. All right. Move along now. Go to work right away."

Al parked the truck close to the door of the little house with number sixty-three on it. The family came down from the truck and stood around looking puzzled. Two policemen approached them. "Name?"

"Joad," Tom said. "What's going on?"

"Now, we don't want any trouble with you. Just do your work and mind your own business and you'll be all right." The two walked away.

After they unloaded the truck, the four men took their buckets and went into the field. "The owner here doesn't waste any time," Tom said. Ruthie and Winfield helped by putting the peaches into boxes. They worked steadily through the afternoon. When Tom finished the twentieth box, he got a credit note for one dollar and took it to Ma. "Here you are. You can get a dollar's worth of stuff at the store."

Ma hurried to the store. She opened the screen door and went in. A tiny man stood behind the counter.

"Good afternoon," Ma said.

"Hi," he said.

"I'd like some meat, please."

"I have all kinds of meat," he said. "Hamburger, twenty cents a pound."

"Ain't that high? It seems to me hamburger was fifteen the last time I got some."

"Well," he laughed softly, "yes, it's high. But if you go into town for a couple of pounds of hamburger, it will cost you about a gallon of gas."

Ma looked at him angrily for a moment. "Ain't you got some cheaper kind of meat?"

"Soup bones," he said. "Ten cents a pound."

"But those are just bones."

"Well, you can go into town and get it for less. A gallon of gas."

"OK," Ma said. "Two pounds of hamburger, a loaf of bread, and five pounds of potatoes, and a bag of coffee. How much is that?"

"That's one dollar exactly," he said.

"What? These are high prices. Who owns this store?"

"Hooper Ranch. But if you want better prices . . ."

"I know, I can go into town." Ma's face was hard as she handed the man her credit note for one dollar.

Tom and Al and Pa and Uncle John walked away from the peach trees. Their feet were a little heavy on the road. Tom said, "Pa, after we eat I'm going to walk out and see what was going on outside that gate. Do you want to come?"

"No," Pa said. "I'm going to rest. I'm tired from all of that picking."

"How about you, Al?"

"I want to look around here first," he said.

"Well, I know Uncle John won't come. I guess I'll go alone."

The dinner was cooking and the Joad house was full of smoke. Ma worked quickly near the fire while Rosasharn rested on a box. The men came in. "Meat, by God!" said Tom. "And coffee. I smell it. I'm sure hungry."

They ate silently and wiped their plates with bread. The children put their plates on the floor and ate like little animals. Tom swallowed the last piece of bread and said, "Do you have any more, Ma?"

"No," she said. "That's all. You made a dollar, and that's a dollar's worth. They charge extra out here."

"I ain't full," said Tom.

"Well, tomorrow you'll work a full day."

Al wiped his mouth. "I guess I'll take a look around."

"Wait, I'll go with you," Tom said. The two walked out of the house together but then went separate ways. Tom walked over to the high wire gate.

A figure stood beside the road. A voice said, "Hello. Who is it? Where are you going?"

"Well, I thought I'd take a walk."

"You'll have to go another way."

"Can't I get out of here?" Tom asked.

"Not tonight you can't. Those crazy troublemakers might get you."

"What troublemakers?"

"You saw them when you came in, didn't you?"

"Well, I saw a bunch of men. I thought it was an accident," Tom said. He then walked away from the gate until the guard couldn't see him. He heard some voices in the distance and hurried off the road into an area full of bushes and tall grass. He climbed over a wire fence and moved down through the thick grass until he came to a stream. Then he followed the voices along the stream. He stopped when he saw a man on a box in front of a tent.

"Good evening," Tom said.

"Who are you? Do you know anybody here?"

"No. I was just going past."

A head appeared from the tent. A voice said, "What's the matter?"

"Casy!" Tom cried. "Casy. What are you doing here?"

"My God. It's Tom Joad! Come on in, Tommy."

"Do you know him?" the man in front asked.

"Yeah, I've known him for years," said Casy. He pulled Tom into the tent.

Three other men sat on the ground in the middle of the tent. One man got up and said, "Glad to meet you. This is the fellow you told us about?"

"Sure. This is him. Where are your folks, Tom? What are you doing here?"

"Well," said Tom, "we heard that there was some work this way. And I saw a bunch of fellows screaming outside the gate. But the guards wouldn't tell us anything. So, I came out here to see what's going on. How did you get here, Casy?"

"A jailhouse is a funny place," the preacher said. "I met lots of men who stole stuff because they couldn't get it any other way. Do you see?"

"No," Tom said.

"Well, maybe I can't tell you. Maybe you have to see for yourself." Casy put his chin on his hands. "How's your sister?"

"She's as big as a cow. But you ain't told me what's going on."

The oldest man said, "This is a strike."

"Well, five cents a box isn't much, but a fellow can eat," Tom said.

"Five cents?" the older man said. A heavy silence fell in the tent.

Casy stared out the entrance. "Tom," he said at last. "We came here to work. They said that it was going to be five cents. But when we got here, it was only two and a half cents. A fellow can't eat on that. So, we said we won't take it. So, they threw us out. Tell your folks, Tom. As soon as we're gone, they'll start paying you two and a half cents."

"Well, I'll try to tell them," Tom said. "It's hard to talk around here with all those guys walking around with guns."

"Tell them, Tom."

The older man said, "Sh. I hear something."

They all listened to the soft sound of footsteps walking near. "Let's go," said Casy. They moved quickly along the edge of the stream.

Then a voice called out, "There they are!" Two flashlight beams fell on the men, caught them, blinded them. "Stand where you are. That's him."

Casy said, "Listen, you fellows don't know what you're doing. You're helping to kill kids."

A heavy man swung a large stick at Casy. The stick crashed into the side of his head and Casy fell sideways out of the light. "Oh God, George, I think you killed him," a voice said.

Tom looked down at the preacher. Then, he jumped silently at the man with the stick and pulled it from his hands. He swung once and hit the man's shoulder. He swung again and hit him hard on the head. The large body sank to the ground. Tom hit his head three more times. There were shouts, the sound of running feet. The flashlights moved up and down. And then a stick reached Tom's head, a blow to the side of his face. He fell to the ground but got up quickly and ran.

He went low along the ground and hid in the tall grass until footsteps went past him. He got up again and found his way to the fence.

He walked silently to the door of the Joad house. The door made a noise as he opened it. And Ma's voice said, "Who's that?"

"Me, Tom."

"Well, you'd better get some sleep."

Tom did not sleep. His wounded face hurt, his broken nose ached with pain. The dawn came finally.

Pa put on his old coat, yawning and stretching. Ma looked over at Tom. "What's the matter?" she said.

"Sh," Tom said. "I got into a fight."

"Tom."

"I couldn't help it, Ma."

"What's the matter?" Uncle John asked.

"What is this?" Pa demanded.

"I found the preacher last night," Tom said.

"The preacher?" Pa asked.

"Yeah. But he was leading a strike and they came for him and they killed him. I was standing there and I went crazy. I hit a guy."

Ma's breath caught in her throat. Pa said softly, "Did you kill him?"

"I don't know," Tom said. "I hope so."

"Tom!" Ma said.

"Oh, you have to know. Casy came out here with other fellows to get five cents. But then they changed it to two and a half cents."

"A fellow can't eat on that."

"And then the pickers went on strike. And now the cops killed Casy."

"Well, we need to get to work." Ma looked sadly at Tom. "Rosasharn will stay with you. We'll tell them that you're sick today."

The family went to work. Tom finally fell asleep. His sister watched him and the door.

As the sun began to set, Ma came back to the house. She carefully built a fire in one end of the stove and filled a pot with water and put it over the flame.

"How was picking today?" Tom asked.

Ma took a cup of dried corn pieces out of a bag. "I don't want to talk about it," she said.

Pa and Al and Uncle John and the children came into the house. Al looked at Ma and said, "Is that all we get after working until dark?"

"Al, you know we have to go. It will take all of the money we have for gas."

"But, Ma, a fellow needs meat if he's going to work."

"Just sit," she said.

They all sat down to their small dinners and coffee. Pa said, "They dropped the price like you said, Tom. Two and a half cents."

Uncle John said, "They say there are two hundred more men coming tonight."

They were silent for a few minutes. Then Pa said, "Tom, it looks like you've done it."

"I thought so."

Uncle John said, "They have men out there looking for you. They said that they're going to kill the man who did it."

"But I only did it after they killed Casy."

"They're saying you started it," Pa said.

Ma cried, "It ain't true!"

Tom said, "Ma, I have to go."

She got to her feet. "You ain't going. We can hide you, and we can bring you something to eat while your face gets well. We'll take you out of here. Al, you back the truck against the door. We'll put the load in and hide Tom underneath some blankets." The family stared at her for a moment. "Come on, it's dark enough. Let's go."

Al drove down the smaller country roads away from the lines of police cars and men on strike. At the edge of the road he saw a sign that said *Cotton Pickers Wanted*. He slowed the car. The family got out and Tom said, "I know a way I can stay with you without getting you into any trouble. There's a small stream just up the road with lots of bushes around it. I can hide there."

"And we can live in one of those boxcars over there, where the pickers live," Ma added.

"As soon as my face is well, I'll come out," Tom said.

"It seems like a good idea to me," said Pa.

Chapter 9 The Cotton Camps

Cotton Pickers Wanted said the signs along the road. People appeared, ready to work. They picked the cotton and put it into large bags. If they did not have a bag, they had to buy one for a dollar. When a bag broke, they sewed up the open end. When both ends broke, they used the cloth to make clothes.

The bags full of cotton were weighed. Sometimes, the scales cheated the cotton pickers of money. Sometimes, the cotton pickers put rocks in the bags to make them heavier. The cotton pickers and the scale man always argued, always fought.

The cars moved into the cotton fields and the cotton camps were set up. The boxcars, twelve of them, stood end to end on a little flat area near the stream. They had large sliding doors but no windows. The Joads shared an end car with the Wainwrights, so Ma hung a large blanket across the middle of the boxcar. The cotton pickers worked quickly until dark each day. They knew the work would soon end.

Ma came into the boxcar carrying a large bag full of food. Rosasharn sat on a box beside the stove. "Did you get milk?" the girl demanded.

"Yeah, right here," Ma said. "Are the potatoes ready?"

"Yeah, Ma."

"Well, we're going to have pork tonight," Ma said with a smile on her face.

Uncle John and Pa and Al came in. Winfield followed behind. "Ma," Winfield said. "Ma, Ruthie told."

"Told what."

"About Tom."

Ma stared at Winfield. "What did she say?"

"She only told a little. A big girl took her candy and Ruthie tried to get it back and they got into a fight. And the big girl said that she was going to get her big brother. And Ruthie said she was going to get her big brother who was hiding because he killed a man."

"Oh!" Ma said. "Oh! Dear God." She looked at Winfield and

said, "You go get Ruthie. Pa, you stay here, and I'll take Tom some food and tell him what's happened."

"All right," Pa agreed.

Ma quickly put some food in a bowl and covered it with a towel. She stepped out of the boxcar and moved proudly down the line of tents and cars. She stepped in among the tall grass and bushes along the stream until she found the cave where Tom was hiding. "Tom," she called.

"Is that you, Ma?"

"Yeah, right over here. I have to talk to you, Tom."

"You have to come in so no one sees you."

She lowered her head and went into the cave. It was dark and she could not see Tom's face. But she knew that he was near. She placed the food down and soon she could hear him chewing. "Ruthie told about you, Tom."

"What? Why did she do that?"

"Well, it wasn't her fault. Some kids were fighting and it came out." Then Ma was silent. She finally said, "You have to go, Tom. I don't want you to."

"I know, Ma."

"How's your face?" She reached out into the darkness and felt his head and face. "You have a bad wound and your nose is all bent."

"Maybe that's a good thing. No one will know me."

"Tom, I have some money for you. Seven dollars. It ain't much. But you can take a bus far away from here."

"Oh, Ma. You need that money."

"Now, you just take it."

"OK," he said. He then ate the rest of the food.

Ma said, "What are you going to do?"

"What Casy did," he said.

"But they killed him."

"Yeah," said Tom. "He didn't run quick enough. He wasn't doing anything against the law. And all of these people are working hard and living like animals."

She put the money in Tom's hand. "Goodbye," she said. She walked away quickly.

"Goodbye," Tom said softly.

When Ma returned to the boxcar, Pa and Uncle John were sitting outside. Ma said, "I found Tom, and I sent him away."

Pa sadly looked away. Uncle John dropped his chin on his chest. Then Pa said, "The cotton's nearly gone."

Al stepped out from the boxcar. Ma said, "We'll have to move along."

"I'll have to go soon," Al said.

"You can't," Ma said. "We need you."

"Well, Aggie Wainwright and me are going to get married and I'm going to get a job in a garage and rent a house. And nobody can stop us."

Pa and Uncle John and Ma stared at him. "Al," Ma said at last. "We're glad. We're very glad."

"You are?"

"Well, you're grown up. And a man needs a wife. But don't go now, Al. Stay until spring."

Mrs. Wainwright's head appeared from the boxcar. "Have you heard the news?"

"Yeah. Just heard," Ma said.

"Well, let's have a little party!"

Rosasharn came to the door of the boxcar. "What's the matter?"

"It's good news!" Ma said. "Al and Aggie are getting married. And we're going to have a little party."

The next day, the rain started. The roads were shiny with water. The rain fell steadily. Hour by hour the cotton plants seemed to blacken and die. The evening came early. The rain continued. In the boxcars the families stayed close together, listening to the pouring water on the roofs. The families knew that this meant no more cotton, no work until spring—no money, no food.

Then pools of water formed and in the low places little lakes formed in the fields. The muddy lakes rose higher. At last, the mountains were full and the hillsides spilled into the streams.

On the third day of the rain, the sound of the stream could be heard above the drumming rain. Pa and Uncle John stood in the open door and looked out over the rising stream.

Uncle John said, "Some fellows are talking about moving somewhere else."

"But these cars are dry," Pa said. "You can't find as dry a place as these cars. You wait." He looked down at the water again. "It's coming up fast. Maybe those other fellows will want to dig an area for the water to go into and a wall to stop it coming over here."

Ma's voice called out, "Mrs. Wainwright, Mrs. Wainwright!"

The fat little woman came down the car. "Do you want me?"

Ma pointed to Rosasharn's face. "Look." The girl's forehead was wet and fear filled her eyes. "I think it's coming. It's early."

Mrs. Wainwright bent over the girl and looked at her carefully. "It will be all right."

Ma said, "Ruthie! You and Winfield go outside with Aggie. Go on now."

"Why?" they demanded.

"Because Rosasharn is going to have her baby. Now go."

Rosasharn said nervously, "Is it coming?"

"Sure," Ma said. "You're going to have a nice baby."

"We'll help you, honey," Mrs. Wainwright said.

Pa put his head in through the narrow opening of the door. "Why did you shut the door?"

Ma said, "Her time's come."

"Then, we have to build that wall. We couldn't go if we wanted to."

"No. We can't go now."

Pa ran outside, stepping heavily through the mud. "We have to build the wall. We can't go now. My girl is having a baby."

Twenty men helped build the wall, digging the mud with shovels and buckets. They worked quickly, like machines. When one man dropped his shovel, another man picked it up and continued shoveling. They took off their coats and hats. Their clothes and shoes were covered in mud.

A scream came from the Joad car. The men stopped and listened anxiously and then went back to work. The water rose slowly up the side of the new wall. "Higher!" Pa cried. "We have to get it higher!"

The evening came and the work went on. And now the men were almost too tired to stand. From time to time Pa looked in the car door. "All right?" he asked.

"Yeah! I think so," Ma said.

The stream was suddenly growing more quickly. Then, from up the stream came a loud crash. A large tree had fallen into the stream and was coming down toward the wall. The tired men watched, their mouths hanging open. The tree pushed and broke the wall. The broken wall washed quickly down, washed around ankles, around knees. The men turned and ran. "Come on, the cars are high," Pa cried.

They ran back to the boxcars. Some of the men hurried into their vehicles and drove off through the mud.

Pa carefully squeezed through the narrow door opening. The two lamps were turned low. Ruthie and Winfield were asleep in the corner. Ma sat on the bed beside Rosasharn. Ma looked up when Pa entered, and then quickly down.

"How is she?" Pa asked.

Ma did not look up again. "All right, I think. Sleeping."

"Never breathed," said Mrs. Wainwright softly. "Never was alive."

Pa said weakly, "We did what we could."

"I know," Ma said.

"We worked all night. And a tree cut through the wall."

"I know," she said.

"I don't know how high the stream's going to rise. It might flood the boxcar. Maybe we'll have to go."

Ruthie moved her hand over her eyes. "Where's the baby?" she demanded.

Ma wet her lips. "There ain't any baby. There never was a baby. We were wrong. Now go back to sleep."

Pa and Al and Uncle John sat in the boxcar doorway and watched the dawn come up. The rain had stopped. But the water was still climbing slowly. "Do you think it will come in the boxcar?" Al asked.

"I don't know."

"Well, I've been thinking. We can take down the sideboards of the truck and build a platform. That way we can pile our stuff up and maybe it will stay dry until the water level goes back down. And we can go across to the other side of the highway, away from the stream water, on higher ground."

Pa thought for a minute. "Yeah. We need to do that. We can't stay here."

"I'll get started," Al said.

The rain began again. Ma built a little fire with the last of the dry sticks. The family sat around and ate the last of their food, boiled potatoes. Finally Pa said, "It's time to go."

Al said, "I can't. Aggie. She and I . . ."

"Of course," Ma said. "You stay here, Al. Take care of our stuff.

When the water goes down, we'll come back. Come on, Rosasharn, children. We're going to a dry place."

Pa and Uncle John hurried out first and stood in the water waiting. They helped Rosasharn, sad and weak. Pa held Rosasharn as high as he could. Uncle John carried Ruthie while Winfield rode on his shoulders. Together they walked slowly to the highway, where the children got down. Ma searched the land and flooded fields with her eyes. Then she saw an old barn. "Come on," she called to her family. "This way."

The rain became heavier. "Hurry up, Ruthie, Winfield. Run ahead."

They entered the old barn. It was dark inside. A little light came in through the cracks in the old boards. Winfield said, "Look! In the corner."

Ma looked. There were two figures, a man who lay on his back, and a boy sitting beside him. The boy looked at them and said, "Do you own this place?"

"No," Ma said. "We've just come in from the rain. We have a sick girl." Ma looked at the man. "What's the matter with him?"

"He got sick in the cotton. Hasn't eaten in six days. Said he wasn't hungry or he just ate. Gave me the food. Now he's too weak to move."

"Is he your pa?" Ma asked.

"Yeah," the boy said. He started to cry. "He's dying. Last night I went and stole some bread but he couldn't eat it. Got to have soup or milk. Do you folks have money for milk?"

Ma said, "Don't worry. We'll think of something." She looked at Pa and Uncle John watching the sick man. She looked at Rosasharn, now sitting on the floor with a blanket wrapped around her. Ma's eyes passed Rosasharn's eyes and then came back to them. And the two women looked deep into each other.

The girl said, "Yes."

Ma smiled. "I knew you would," she said.

Rosasharn whispered, "Will—will you all go out?"

Ma reached out and brushed the hair from her daughter's forehead and then kissed her. She said to the others, "Come on, let's go outside for a few minutes." She took the boy's arm and stepped outside the barn. Uncle John, Pa, and the children followed her.

For a minute, Rosasharn sat quietly. Then, she raised her tired body and went over to the dying man. She stood looking down at the thin face, into the wide frightened eyes. Then, slowly she lay down beside him. He shook his head slowly from side to side. Rosasharn loosened one side of the blanket and let out her breast. "You have to," she said and pulled his head close. "There!" she said. "There." Her hand moved behind his head and supported it. Her fingers moved gently in his hair. She looked up and across the barn and smiled mysteriously.

ACTIVITIES

Chapters 1–3

Before you read

1 Look at the Word List at the back of this book.

a Which of these words refer to vehicles or parts of a vehicle?

appendix headlight parole tractor windshield

b Which of these words refer to people?

barn fellow folks pauper preacher reverend tenant

2 The word "ain't" has a number of meanings. Which of these meanings does it have in the sentences below?

hasn't haven't isn't aren't am not

a "I ain't heard lately."

b "That ain't my business."

c "Ain't you young Tom Joad?"

d "Well, I ain't going."

3 Read the Introduction to this book. Then answer these questions.

a When did Wall Street, the financial center of the U.S., crash?

b Who did people blame for the Depression?

c What were people from the Dust Bowl looking for in California?

d Why were Californians unwelcoming?

e Why was *The Grapes of Wrath* criticized by some people when it came out?

f Which prize did John Steinbeck win for this book?

While you read

4 Read Chapter 1. Are these sentences right (✓) or wrong (✗)?

a The truck driver has a *No Riders* sign in his truck. .....

b He gives a ride to the man who is walking along the highway. .....

c The hitchhiker's father owns a farm. .....

d Tom Joad has been in prison. .....

e Reverend Casy recognizes Tom. .....

- **f** Tom has been in prison for seven years. .....
- **g** Casy is still a preacher. .....
- **h** The Joads' house looks the same as when Tom left. .....

5 Write the correct name on. Who:

- **a** meets Tom and Reverend Casy at the Joad family's house? ....
- **b** has gone to Uncle John's house? ....
- **c** has been picking cotton? ....
- **d** has destroyed the tenants' houses? ....
- **e** has gone to California? ....
- **f** hasn't eaten fresh meat for years? ....
- **g** comes to find trespassers? ....
- **h** hides in a cave? ....

6 Read Chapter 2. Circle the correct words.

- **a** One man on a tractor can take the place of fourteen *men / families*.
- **b** Uncle John's wife died from a *stomachache / burst appendix*.
- **c** Pa thinks that Tom has *escaped / been paroled* from prison.
- **d** If Tom leaves the state, the police will send him back *to prison / home*.
- **e** Ma recognizes Tom *immediately / eventually*.
- **f** Tom's older brother *Noah / Al* doesn't speak much.
- **g** His sister Rosasharn is going to *get married / have a child*.
- **h** Ma puts cough medicine in Grandpa's coffee to make him *feel better / sleep*.

7 Read Chapter 3. Put these sentences in the correct order, from 1–8.

- **a** After chewing on pork bones, everybody gets back in the truck. .....
- **b** The Joads bury Grandpa and leave a note with his name on it. .....

c The Joads meet the Wilsons when they stop to camp for the night. .....

d Ma tells Tom she is worried about him crossing the state line. .....

e Grandpa dies inside the Wilsons' tent. .....

f Tom suggests that the Wilsons travel with the Joads. .....

g The man at the gas station asks Al if he has money to pay for the gas. .....

h Al stops the truck because Grandma wants to get out. .....

After you read

8 How have these changed since Tom went to prison?

a Casy

b the Joads' house

c Muley Graves

d Pa

e Al

9 Who is speaking? What are they talking about?

a "I like it here. I feel like no one can get me."

b "I have the papers right here."

c "I don't want any stupid oranges or grapes."

d "We're paying our own way."

e "Maybe they have crimes in California that we don't even know about."

f "If I could only fix a car, but I don't know anything about cars."

Chapters 4–5

Before you read

10 Look at the Contents page and read the titles of Chapters 4 and 5. What do you think is going to happen in the chapters?

11 Do you think the Joads and the Wilsons will get to California and find work? Why (not)?

While you read

12 Match the names with the sentence endings.

a Rosasharn…	goes crazy.
b Connie…	refuses to break up the family.
c Tom and Casy...	doesn't want to live in the country.
d Ma...	wants to study and have a store.
e Grandma…	stay behind to repair the car.

13 Are these sentences true (T) or false (F)?

a Tom quickly takes the broken part off the car. .....
b They need a part for a 1931 Dodge. .....
c They buy the part for thirty-five cents. .....
d The campsite costs fifty cents for each vehicle. .....
e The ragged man is on his way to California. .....
f Tom stops Pa from telling Ma what the ragged man said. .....

14 Complete the sentences with these names of places.

Oklahoma Barstow jail Colorado River desert

a After the Joads cross the .... , they are in California.
b Poor people from .... are called "Oakies."
c The policeman threatens to put Ma and her family in .... if he finds them there the next evening.
d The guard at the inspection station tells Ma that she can find a doctor for Grandma in ....
e When they finally get across the .... , the Joads see the green valley with rows of fruit trees.

After you read

15 Discuss with another student why these events surprise the Joads.

a Ma says, with a hammer in her hand, "I ain't going."
b The ragged man tells Pa and the others about the men who print the handbills.
c Pa and then Ma learn the word "Oakie."
d Ma tells the family that Grandma is dead.

16 Work with another student and have this conversation.

Student A: You are Noah and you have decided not to go on with the family. Tell Tom and explain why.

Student B: You are Tom. Try to persuade Noah not to leave the family.

Chapters 6–7

Before you read

17 Discuss these questions.

- **a** Do you think that Noah has made a good decision? Will Ma try to find him and bring him back? Will anyone else leave the family?
- **b** How will life in a Hooverville change the Joads?

While you read

18 Answer these questions. Write Yes or No.

- **a** Are there many Hoovervilles? .....
- **b** Does Grandma have a nice funeral? .....
- **c** Do sheriffs want to prevent Oakies from voting? .....
- **d** Does Connie regret leaving Oklahoma? .....
- **e** Does Floyd think that the contractor is dishonest? .....

19 Are these people telling the truth or a lie? Write the letters, a–e.

The truth: .... Lies ....

- **a** "He looks like one of the guys wanted for stealing a car just last week," said the sheriff.
- **b** "They'll fingerprint you. You broke parole. They'll send you back," Casey whispered to Tom.
- **c** "I knocked out your man there," Casy told the police.
- **d** "We were just playing," Ruthie told Tom.
- **e** "Connie will find us..." Tom told Rosasharn.

20 Complete these sentences.

a Timothy Wallace works for ....

b The Wallaces had to sell their car for ....

c The Farmers' Association pays workers ....

d The police will go into the government camp if ....

e The Joad children have never seen ....

f The police can't go into the camp because ....

After you read

21 Discuss these questions.

a What does Tom learn about the police, the Bank of the West, and the government camps?

b What is happening to each person in the Joad family as they search for work?

Chapters 8–9

Before you read

22 Discuss these questions.

a Will the Joads stay at the government camp? Why (not)?

b How will the story end for each of the main characters?

While you read

23 Write the missing words in these sentences.

a The banks and companies that own the large farms also own the .... factories.

b They paid .... low wages.

c They made the price of .... go down.

d The .... farmers couldn't sell their fruit.

e The fruit was ....

24 Are these dreams (D) or facts (F) in the story?

a Rosasharn would have plenty of milk if Connie were with her. .....

b There is work picking peaches at the Hooper Ranch. .....

c Al is going to get a job at a garage, live in a nice room, and eat well. .....

d Tom fills twenty boxes and gets a credit note for one dollar. .....

e Hooper Ranch owns the store where Ma buys hamburger. .....

f Tom enjoys meat and coffee for supper after their first day working on the Hooper Ranch. .....

g Ma will have more money for food on their second day there because Tom will work a full day. .....

25 What happens after Tom talks to the guard about the trouble-makers? Match the two halves of these sentences.

a Tom meets his old friend Casy, ...

b One of the men with flashlights is a heavy man named George, ...

c Tom angrily attacks George, ...

d Tom doesn't see the man ... .

1) who hits him before he manages to run away.

2) who is one of the striking troublemakers at Hooper Ranch.

3) who falls and dies after he is hit on the head.

4) who kills Casy with a large stick.

26 Write the missing word in these sentences.

a The Joads and the Wainwrights live in the same ....

b Tom hides in a dark .... until Ruthie tells a girl about his crime.

c After three days of rain, the .... rises dangerously high.

d Twenty men help Pa to build a .... but it is destroyed by a fallen tree.

e The Joads cross the highway to higher ground and find shelter inside a dark ....

After you read

27 Answer these questions.

a Why do the Joads leave the government camp?

b Why are the police outside the Hooper Ranch?

c How does Tom find Casy?

d What reasons are suggested for the death of Rosasharn's baby?

e What does Rosasharn do at the end of the story?

28 Who is speaking? What are they talking about?

a "It's nice here. The folks are nice."

b "Now just one each. That's all we have."

c "It's not your business. Do you want to work?"

d "If you want better prices . . ."

e "A fellow can't eat on that."

f "I was standing there and I went crazy."

g "As soon as my face is well, I'll come out."

h "Ma, Ruthie told."

i "I think it's coming. It's early."

j "Will—will you all go out?"

29 The story shows both how cruel and how kind people can be to each other in desperate circumstances. Discuss which scenes show the greatest cruelty and which show the greatest generosity.

Writing

30 Imagine that you are a landowner in the Dust Bowl in 1939. Write a letter to one of your tenant farmers explaining why he and his family must leave their home.

31 Make a list of things that the Joads should take with them when they leave their house and begin their journey to California in 1939. Add a reason why each is important.

32 Imagine that you are Ruthie and Winfield, ten years later. What do you remember most about your trip to California? Write some of your memories for your children to read.

33 Compare life in the government camp at Weedpatch and life in the Hooverville. How do you think they compare with camps for migrants today?

34 Write Ma's diary for the days after Tom leaves to the end of the story. Write the day's main events and her feelings about what happened.

35 After the story ends, what do you think happens next to the members of the Joad family? Write a short additional chapter for the book.

36 Write a letter to a friend about this book. Write about the story. Did you like it? Did you learn from it? Why (not)?

37 Write about the injustices experienced by the migrant workers in this story. Do migrant workers today suffer in the same way? Find one or two personal stories in the newspapers or on the Internet to use as examples.

38 Choose one or two characters from the story and describe their personalities. Explain what you would have done differently if you had been them, and give your reasons.

39 How does poverty change a person, a family, and a society? What is society's responsibility to the poor? Write about your views for a newspaper or magazine, with reference to your own country.

WORD LIST

ain't (v) a non-standard short form of *am not*, *is not*, *are not*, *has not* or *have not*

appendix (n) a small part of your body that has little or no use but can cause serious harm if it bursts

barn (n) a large building on a farm for keeping crops and sometimes animals in

boxcar (n) a railroad car with high sides and a roof that is used for carrying goods

committee (n) a group of people chosen to do a particular job, or to make decisions

cop (n) an informal word for a police officer

coroner (n) an official who examines bodies to find the cause of sudden or unexpected deaths

diner (n) a small restaurant that serves inexpensive meals

fellow (n) an informal word for a man

fist (n) a hand with all the fingers bent tightly in

folks (n pl) an informal word for people; "my folks" are a person's family

handbill (n) a small, printed advertising sheet of paper that is given to people by hand

headlight (n) one of the large lights at the front of a vehicle

horizon (n) the place where the land or sea seems to meet the sky

migrant (n) a person who regularly moves from one area to another

parole (n) permission to leave prison on condition that you behave well

pauper (n) an old-fashioned word for someone who is very poor

peach (n) a round, juicy, yellow-red fruit with a large rough seed and a soft skin

porch (n) a roof, with a floor but no walls, built onto the outside of a house at the entrance

preacher (n) someone who talks about religious subjects, usually in a church

ragged (adj) old, dirty, and in bad condition
reverend (n) a minister in the Christian church
rust (n) the red-brown substance that forms on wet metal
tenant (n) someone who pays rent to the owner for land or rooms
tractor (n) a strong vehicle with large wheels, used for pulling farm equipment
trespass (v) to go onto someone else's land without permission
unit (n) a group of people who are part of a larger group
wage (n) the amount of money that you earn, usually for an hour of work
windshield (n) the large window at the front of a car
wrath (n) a formal word for very great anger